LIFE WAS
A CABARET

LIFE WAS
A CABARET

Jana —

Congratulations on landing the best galley slave on any ocean.
Love
Laura

Becky
Coffield

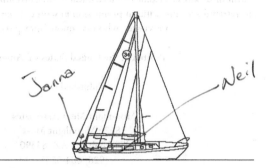

Jonna

Neil

LIFE
WAS A
CABARET

MOONLIGHT MESA ASSOCIATES
Wickenburg, Arizona

Published by:

Moonlight Mesa Associates
18620 Moonlight Mesa
Wickenburg, AZ. 85390
(928) 684-5235
www.moonlightmesaassociates.com

Distributed in North America by:

**R. Hale & Co. Inc.
Nautical Book Distributors
1803 132nd Avenue, N.E. Suite 4
Bellevue, WA. 98005-2261
425-881-5212; 800-733-5330**

Cover photo of Cabaret in Pokai Bay by Robert Kemmler

Cover design by Jack W. Davis www.jackdavis.com

Library of Congress Control Number 2005938332

For my husband Tom, who made
this journey possible.

CONTENTS

CONTENTS

ACKNOWLEDGEMENTS

For at least a decade after my husband and I returned from our adventure, I was asked by friends and family, many times, when this book would be in print. I always rolled my eyes and shrugged in answer. I had good reasons why the project was stalled, really. Details like children, a teaching career, and helping my husband in his business led the list. But then there came a day, children grown, resignation in, when out of the very distant past a person appeared who simply asked, "Did you ever publish your book?" I looked into her soft, kind eyes, and I resolved in that precise moment that this book would come to life, once and for all. And so to Ruby Sharman, I need to say thank you, but a simple thank you just does not seem adequate for reigniting my dream and my enthusiasm for this venture.

I owe a thank you to my uncle, Bill Sharman, for pestering me repeatedly about this project, and for believing that it was not only possible, but expected of me.

Thank you to Tom MacDannold—publisher, author and professor—for his support and advice.

Without the help of my distributor, Seaworthy Publications and my red-penned editor/proof-reader/friend Yvonne Angiola, however, this project still would never have made it off my hard drive. To both of them I say a heartfelt thank you.

This is a story of an adventure—perhaps the greatest of my life. And so I owe a final thanks to my husband Tom, without whom this adventure could never have happened. He was there with me, when life was indeed a Cabaret.

Becky Coffield

SECOND THOUGHTS

I DOUBT I WILL EVER LEARN as much about myself again as I did on my first ocean passage from Acapulco to Nuku Hiva, now almost three decades ago. It was February, 1981. For twenty-seven days I had plenty of time to think—my husband Tom and I both did—and perhaps we came to decisions and conclusions that we might never have made had we not taken such a block of time and, without interruption or distractions, thought each thing out in every aspect. On the other hand, perhaps our situation tainted our thinking. Will I ever know?

Our passage began beautifully enough in light winds, calm seas and Acapulco blue skies. For the first week I pinched myself daily and gloated over the fact that yes, I did have the courage to make a crossing. I had always wondered if at the last minute as land faded from view I wouldn't "freak out" and, head hung low, bump my way back up Baja and the thousand miles of coastline home. Thus, my first mistake was to equate ocean crossings with courage. Since my first crossing I have learned that any fool can cross an ocean…in fact we met many: People who set off in unseaworthy boats or people with no knowledge of navigation. Anyway, every day I smirked in smug exhilaration over the fact that here I was making a passage at last.

1

We soon found ourselves developing a simple routine. We ran four hour watches beginning at dark. (On later crossings we changed to three hour watches as the fourth hour is deadly for the one on watch in the middle of the night.) During the day we did not run a formal watch, for one of us was usually outside reading or "butt bathing", an activity that consisted of laying across our deck box with our bare butts exposed to the sun to help control the saltwater sores that one tends to develop from long stretches of sitting in slightly soggy, salted clothes. Anyway, I tended to be outside more due to my claustrophobia, while Tom found himself a nest below to burrow into. At noon I took a sun shot which Tom plotted along with his DR (dead reckoning—a guesstimate at where one is based on speed, direction, time, and current) and then we had our bathing hour. This finished, we opened the "casino" and played cribbage, the only game we had where the pieces didn't slide all over the board. We gambled for a dollar a game and dish duty the next day. Let me only say that by Nuku Hiva Tom had dishpan hands and owed me $35,000 which, I might add, he denies and has never even attempted to pay me. After the dinner hour we began our watches. Tom frequently took star shots in the evening, and he became quite familiar with many stars. At least I think he did, but how would I know since I only recognize a few! Unfortunately, despite the hours I spent on watch with *Field Guide to the Stars and Planets,* I learned no more about the stars than I'd known when we left Oregon some three years earlier. Other than the northern basics, I'm afraid to admit that they all just looked the same to me!

March 6th was a cloudy day, but the barometer was holding and we had no rational reason for concern. In fact, it was a relief to escape the sun's murderous heat for a day. We even had a rainstorm pass over and happily collected gallons of water; we topped off our water tank, filled two teapots, refilled our sun shower and filled up various pots and pans. At 5:15, however, the reason for my growing unease became apparent. A blast of wind from the northeast struck *Cabaret* with such force that the boat was almost knocked down. We had been moving along comfortably at five knots with jib and reefed main—suddenly we were on our ear and going over fast. I scrambled out to release the jib sheet which gave a modicum of relief. Amid the increasing wind and rain we lowered the jib and set about double reefing the main. "So this must be a genuine squall, huh, Tom?" I nervously asked. We decided after a few seconds of still increasing heel just to drop the main since we were running water over the rail even in the process of double reefing it. I flipped the autopilot off and headed *Cabaret* downwind. Under bare poles we were now making seven knots and the wind was still increasing. The rigging began its horrible howling and rain crashed down. Tom went below to don raingear while I kept *Cabaret* headed 180 degrees. My smug sense of adventure was quickly fading and was rapidly being replaced by a growing terror. This wasn't in any of the books I'd read! The wind was still steadily accelerating. Our anemometer was frequently hitting fifty-five knots and still stronger gusts screamed past us. The boat was running at eight knots now and, of course, darkness had descended with the storm, leaving me alone with wind and rain beating me from all sides. I decided then and there that darkness was not a comfort on a stormy night at sea.

Tom took over the wheel upon his return and dourly commented, "This is no squall, and this is no gale!" I numbly agreed.

"Do you think this is a hurricane?"

"No."

"Well, how would you know? You've never been in one!" I angrily shouted.

He steered while I sat in the cockpit and eyeballed the growing seas. I was too frightened to stay alone below although I did duck into the cabin once to scan my Bowditch to see if we weren't in fact in a genuine hurricane. Somehow I actually managed to read the chapter while being wildly buffeted about, but Tom was right—it was no hurricane. At best I thought it to be a tropical depression, for which I now had unlimited respect. I did not stay below for long, for I wanted to be with Tom if anything happened...like the boat pitch poling, turning turtle, sinking, things like that. I was now ter-rified and wishing I was crawling up the coast of Baja with my head hung low. *Cabaret* was racing under bare poles at nine knots and surfing to fourteen knots down swells. I had read of boats doing this but never believed it could happen to us. Still the wind kept up its incessant screaming and the seas grew. "Tom, I'm so scared," I wailed piteously. Deep down I felt that if I just verbalized my fear it would all go away.

"So am I." This I did not want to hear from my fearless husband.

"Tom, what's going to happen?" No answer. We both were think-ing the same thing now. We could be killed out here. Why hadn't I considered this possibility earlier? In our youthful exuberance and confidence we had not even bought a life raft! We could die for this lark we were on, and what were we proving anyway? Why hadn't I asked myself if I was willing to pay with my life? All good questions that I had not asked when we started out. We were now in imminent danger. Never had we seen such wind, and I do not say this lightly. We had been in gales; we had made record runs both up and down the Oregon/Washington coasts due to heavy weather and seas. We had been in anchorages—one in Port Orford, Oregon, and one at Bahia de Navedad, Mexico—with winds gusting to sixty. But here, where there was no shore we could possibly swim to, where there was no lifeboat we could turn to, where I felt nothing but a cold sweat and rumblings in my stomach, I realized I was not brave, and just maybe I was not a real sailor.

We watched our backstay do a crazy jig of its own, independent of the hula hoop action of the mast and we both regretted we had not bought the $85 cable cutters we'd seen. What would we do if our mast came off? Why didn't we have a ham radio so I could call someone and tell them where we were…or say goodbye? I found myself thinking about what I'd say, and I feared I would cry and plead for help, and I would not be brave. Or, maybe I would pull through on the radio. I would tell people how much I loved them and that they could be proud of me. Why was I tormenting myself with my melodramas? I have always been prone to theatrics, and here I was in danger of actually dying playing out my death scene and weeping at my own brilliant performance. Maybe it was better we didn't have a radio, but maybe if we'd have had a weather fax we'd have been able to outmaneuver the storm. A lot of maybes; a lot of hindsight.

Out of my reverie I heard Tom hollering, "This isn't worth it, Becky."

"I agree." Somewhat abashedly then, "Are you praying?" We both were. Could I become even more of a hypocrite before the night was over?

The waves were breaking now, and I watched the white curling, foaming seas approach us from what seemed like every angle. Suddenly I cried out, but it was too late. A huge curler broke next to the starboard stern quarter and a wall of water cascaded into the cockpit. Madly I began bailing, wishing our scuppers were ten times their four bit size. In my frenzy I threw out a bucket of Tom's underwear that had been gently agitating in soapy water all afternoon. Three times during the night I bailed our never before swamped cockpit.

I wanted to cry, somehow hoping this childish emotion would make all the trouble go away, but I knew tears would upset Tom, and me, even more. I tried to push out a few just to see though, but my eyes remained dry, as did my mouth.

We alternated wheel wrestling, for neither of us felt confident enough to "lash the helm" and go have a cup of coffee below. I really wonder about people who say they do that. They'll never convince me that they're all that nonchalant. At 11:00 *Cabaret* was still skidding along doing ten to twelve knots, and I had by then set a new personal record for sustained terror. I wondered in passing if in the morning I would discover a full head of white hair in place of my light brown. Off watch we both were so exhausted that we miraculously slipped into a deep sleep lying in the cockpit of the boat in pouring rain, in inches of water, using a wet towel as a pillow. Even a few seconds respite refreshed us. I wondered how I could possibly be so humdrum as to be sleepy on what might very well prove to be my last night alive, but sleep came instantaneously. The one on the wheel would stay with it until eyes could no longer focus on the compass. Often we would begin nodding off while trying to steer. I have no idea how long our times at the wheel were; it may have been ten minutes—it may have been an hour.

Still alive by 2:00 a.m. we both began to feel a sense of survival. We were making it, and by 3:00 there was no question that the storm was abating. *Cabaret* was still under bare poles, but her speed was now only seven knots and seemed to be dropping steadily. Within the hour we were flopping about at three knots and the seas were much less intimidating. Although there were still curlers, none came on board.

Daylight found us trying to motor but having difficulty maneuvering the boat. We had had difficulty steering all night but had thought it was just the storm. Unbeknownst to us our steering vane's cables had jumped their tracks and fouled. In lumpy seas we had to drop the rudder off the vane and haul it aboard. We were wet, tired, and literally a thousand miles from nowhere, but we had survived. Tom had me feel a walnut sized lump on the back of his head where he had slipped and had knocked himself out on one of his forays below. His head ached for a week. Our new American flag was in tatters. We were beaten, but alive.

It was not until much later in the day that I completely broke down. I remember sitting at the settee, looking up and seeing Tom.

Suddenly I realized how much I loved him and that it was my insistence that had brought us on this adventure and threatened his life. The fear I had contained all night arose and I found myself shaking in fright. I was experiencing what I later came to call "reverse claustrophobia", or agoraphobia. The hugeness, the emptiness of the horizon put me on the edge of profound and terrifying hysteria. I told Tom, "Tom, please talk to me. Tell me we're okay and that everything's all right, please!" Tom reassured me, but I don't think he ever understood the brink I almost fell from. The remainder of the trip in traditional winds could not alleviate my anxiety....what if it happened again, only worse?

My fears were not unfounded. Three days out of Nuku Hiva we were hit by the worst squalls and thunder and lightning storms I could ever imagine. Simultaneously the Tuomotus were experiencing hurricane force winds, and the Society Islands were being buffeted by one of the worst storms they'd ever had. We were within feet of being struck by lightning, and I will never forget the look of sheer terror on Tom's face when I flew to the hatch just seconds after the blinding flash and deafening boom had struck. The air was thick with a horrible smell, and our mouths tasted bloody and metallic. I donned my raingear and sat by him, not wanting to leave him alone to the intolerable ravages of nature. We sat there, becalmed in the ensuing downpour, and I held his hand while he struggled with the fear born by the lightning that had struck perhaps fifty feet from the boat. I know now it was a miracle we were not hit.

Going into Nuku Hiva the last three days was tedious for our exhausted nerves. We alternated between flat calm and gusts of Force 8. It was impossible to carry sail to satisfy both extremes. On one occasion I was on watch when a severe squall hit us. We'd been making two or three knots under storm sail alone when suddenly we were up to eight and going over fast. Numbly I stared at the storm sail sheet and wondered if I should release it or let it be. I was so tired I could not make up my mind whether I was over-reacting to the situation or whether we were in real danger. I held the sheet in my hand just debating. Within seconds Tom was at the companionway. Casting one critical glance at the menacingly pumping, bending mast he dove to release the sheet. The wind had actually been driving *Cabaret* to submarine. Our mast, 3/16 aluminum—the mast off the Cal 46—was no lightweight stick. Finally, out of exhaustion, we began motoring. This was an interminable ordeal now, and at times

I gritted my teeth wondering if the distance between us and land would ever diminish.

Our last evening out it began clearing. We raised sail once again and continued until we were within what we felt was twenty-five or thirty miles of the island. We had not had a shot in three days because of cloud cover, so we were hesitant to approach too much closer lest our DR be off due to currents. We did not want to miss land at this point! We hove to and tried to sleep until daybreak, but long before dawn Tom was able to identify one bank of clouds as definitely an island. At daybreak Nuku Hiva lay some twenty miles dead ahead. Too impatient to try and sail in the now light easterly winds, we fired up our engine and headed in. Ten miles from the island we heard *Cabaret* being called on the VHF. We answered the call to find that the *Shannon Marie*, a boat that had left Acapulco the same day we did, had been anxiously awaiting our arrival—fearful lest we'd disappeared in the storm. They had arrived the day before. Later they told us that they had managed to keep a reefed main up in the storm and had made two hundred sixty six miles in twenty-four hours. In so doing, however, they had torn their chain plates loose and had numerous steering difficulties. First they'd sheared the bronze pin in the steering quadrant, and then the whole quadrant blew apart. They had been very concerned about us, and we too had wondered how they'd fared.

So, our first passage came to a close. We had made it, but what damage we had done to ourselves. It would be years before sailing would really be the enchanting activity we'd once thought. Being confined for twenty-seven days had been almost more than either of us could stand. We'd gone through two terrible storms that had definitely eliminated starry thoughts of cruising forever! We'd experienced a profound midway depression (not uncommon, however) and we'd wrestled with thoughts and fears we'd never known before. And now, worst of all, we knew we had two more passages awaiting us—the one to Hawaii, and the one home.

We talked with other boaters and none felt as strongly as we did, but only a very few had had their butts kicked across the Pacific Ocean. Even those unfortunate souls who'd come from Panama and had taken fifty-five and sixty days to reach the Marquesas had not minded the time confined aboard so much, therefore I suspect that a lot of our displeasure at being cooped up was due to our particular chemistry. We both had missed plain old physical activity. But we had definitely formulated some future goals; goals that would change our lives more than ever upon our return. By Nuku Hiva we had no doubt we'd never be world cruisers, leastwise not at this time in our lives. I was actually very glad, however, that we'd done what we were doing when we were doing it, for I could imagine nothing more disheartening than to spend my whole life dreaming about cruising only to find that it just was not what I'd thought it would be. However, the twenty-seven days had not come to naught. I felt we'd learned some valuable things about ourselves and cruising (like don't believe the weather pilot charts!). But it was so disheartening to find we were not sailors in the true sense. Passage making did not seem to be in our blood. I was perhaps better adapted to the confines and adventure of the boat than Tom, but I wasn't going to cruise without him! Coastal cruising and our adventures in Alaska and Mexico notwithstanding, it was sad to admit we were just not in our element at sea. I understood why Robin Graham had headed to Montana after his circumnavigation. I deeply envied the likes of Bernard Moitessier, the Pardeys, and the Smeettens, but I knew we would not be following in their steps, at least at this time. Yet these twenty-seven days may have been the most character building, confidence enhancing, and self awareness developing experience of our young lives. We had made a rugged passage, yes, but we had survived and had, in reality, enjoyed a lot of the trip despite our nights of terror. Twenty odd years later we are still trying to unravel the mystery of our hearts and our love and attraction for sailboats and the sea. In fact, our whole involvement in sailing is rather a mystery in itself when I really think about it!

CABARET IS CONCEIVED

THE IDEA OF OWNING a sailboat first occurred to us over a pitcher of Margaritas on our honeymoon. Tom and I were at Lake Shasta, California, enjoying the dog days of summer before school recalled us to our teaching jobs. We were still dodging whizzing speedboats in a 14' Lido, which we had learned to maneuver pretty deftly. We knew then that the owner of our speedy little craft would soon be returning from Boston and would either want the boat back or want it bought. Of course the thought of buying it was not out of the question, particularly as those early naïve days of marriage indicated that we might really be rolling in the dough. My finagling and figuring indicated we'd be at least $300 richer each month just in rent and utility savings alone. Two can live as cheaply as one in that respect. But as the large pitcher of Margaritas visibly diminished, our thoughts and figures became ever more expansive.

"Really, Tom, why don't we just go and buy a small boat?" Anything seemed possible then. "We could moor it on the Columbia, and then we could go sailing any time and we wouldn't have to trailer it around—but we could get a trailer for it if we wanted," I added as a sage afterthought. This seemed like such a brilliant idea, only to be followed by a better. "Or we could get one with a little cabin and spend weekends and holidays on it!"

9

This was even more agreeable to Tom, who is ever agreeable anyway. We fussed momentarily over what a boat like this might cost, but felt no real intimidation, for after all we had a double income and soon both of our student loans would be paid off and that would amount to an extra grand total of $60 a month! As the night waned and our conversation became increasingly animated, we drew lovelier and more fun-filled adventures with our soon-to-be boat: summers spent roaming the length of the river, maybe even trips to the ocean. And all it would really need was a place to sleep and a tiny cooking area.

Incredible, but true, we had no idea whatsoever what a boat like the one we had in mind would cost. We kept reassuring ourselves that it wouldn't be much because a fellow teaching friend had told us of a guy he knew (you got it) who knew a guy who was casually walking down the docks at Shilshole Marina in Seattle one day when he saw a man who appeared to be utterly disgusted with his boat. The disgusted man promptly sold the boat to the passerby for a mere $6,000…and it was a 32' Erickson. So we reasoned that a tiny boat with an even tinier cabin would probably not cost more than one or two thousand dollars.

"Tom, why don't we, instead of spending $2,000 on something small, go ahead and invest five or six thousand or, well, no more than eight thousand in a *big* boat, and then we could live on it and pay it off and it wouldn't be any different from paying rent."

Was Tom hesitant? I don't remember, for at this time in Oregon such an idea was so revolutionary that even I was startled by it. While people have for years, we found out much later, lived aboard boats in California and maybe Washington, I can say almost uncategorically that such a thing was very rare in Oregon in 1975. Unlike California, Oregon does not have a very conducive climate for year around living aboard. Unlike Washington and California both, Oregon does not have a fraction of the mooring facilities. Most of the moorages along the Columbia River at that time were not even capable of handling very large boats. But in August, 1975, as Tom and I climbed into our Lake Shasta cabin bed, the idea of living aboard a sailboat was rapidly germinating, although the thought had only an hour before been planted. We were both excited beyond belief, for our plan seemed so simple, so sure, so perfect we could hardly contain our excitement.

"Do you think it's possible?"

"Won't people have a fit when they hear about this?"

"Do you think it will be too small to move around in?"

"Do you think we can buy one for $6,000?"

"Where do you buy these things anyway?"

These questions and thousands of others were asked by each of us over the course of the next few hours, days, and months. The fact that we didn't really even know where to begin looking for such a boat is indicative of the total lack of knowledge the two of us shared regarding sailboats. My husband might have known a sloop from a ketch from a yawl and a schooner, but I had no idea what anything but a Lido was. Under such circumstances, *Cabaret* was conceived.

With this newly hatched dream in mind, the prospect of returning to school seemed not as bleak as formerly anticipated. If we could just live on one salary and save the other, we could actually pay cash for it in no time, and in such an expansive mood we decided we could go as high as $10,000.

We began spending Saturdays and Sundays prowling about the docks of Portland, but we neither saw what we wanted nor, since we'd never been on a big boat, knew what exactly we were looking for. We learned very quickly, however, certain modes of ship-buying behavior. We learned that docks are apparently sacrosanct to many boat owners, so one should look like one has a purpose on the docks and is not a sightseer. Thus, if we acted like we belonged there and knew what we were doing we were rarely bothered or asked what our business was. Rule two was to always check for a lock on the cabin door before one began inspecting a boat. Inspection in our case involved staring dumbly at the various items and taking a mental note of them. We would comment aloud from time to time to impress any happenstance passerby.

Of course our biggest lesson was to come several weeks later, when we first stepped into a broker's office. Our lack of experience must have been obvious, as must our pie in the sky attitude.

"What kind of boat are you looking for?" the black-haired man brusquely asked.

"Well...we aren't really sure yet. Something a person could live aboard though, maybe 30 to 35 feet," Tom answered. I felt strangely conspicuous and intimidated.

"How much money you prepared to spend?" Another whack at my insecurity.

"Well, we haven't really decided yet." I was feeling humiliated. I could not believe the nerve of this brass person asking such questions. I'd been brought up that one didn't ask personal financial questions and here this man was asking us about money right off the bat. I was furious.

"You'd better be prepared to spend $1,000 a foot for a boat in that size range," he said matter of factly.

"For a used boat even?" Gulp.

"Yes. You don't save much money buying used." Fortunately, other people were waiting and his attention quickly leapt to another victim as we mumbled our thanks and slunk out the door.

In the car we were positively sputtering in outrage and disbelief. $1,000 a foot! That meant we'd be paying $30,000 or $35,000! That was unheard of!

"That crass creature obviously doesn't know what he's talking about!" I all but shouted. "Tom, remember that guy who got that boat for $6,000? I know we can find one if we just keep looking!" We resolved we'd never buy a boat from that dealer, no matter what.

We were both angry and upset. $35,000! We'd noticed a list of used boats on his chalkboard, however, and one had been for $15,000…which suddenly didn't seem so unreasonable, so we set off in search again.

That weekend culminated with the end of our search for a boat in Portland. We'd spent the better part of the fall combing docks and had arrived at two conclusions: one, our boat was not in Portland; two, we had to start reassessing our idea of what the boat might cost. We realized by the end of October that even if we did find our boat we couldn't afford it anyway. And we felt our odds of being in the right place at the right time to pick up a $6,000 bonanza were not very realistic. As yet we didn't even have $6,000.

But our time on the docks of Portland had taught us many things. We were schooled now in the art of the right questions. We had learned that if we were to be taken seriously we had to know what questions to ask, and it helped if the seller or broker thought we had previously owned a boat. (Well, there was Tom's duck hunting scow!) So we routinely began by saying we were looking for a 30 to 35 foot fiberglass boat with a diesel engine, but we were not set on how it was rigged. Then we'd discuss the pro's and con's of full keels versus fin keels along with a myriad of sailboat nuances from types of cooking stoves, to tillers versus wheels, to large cockpits versus small. We learned very quickly that each item under discussion had its proponents and its opponents. One guy loved fin keels; another would not consider going offshore with one. It was an endless jumble of fact, opinion, lore, and belief. We consumed everything we were told as if we were at a Roman orgy, then later we carefully digested the bits of information we had gleaned.

Finally, the weekend came—we would take our search to Seattle. My infrequent visits there had taught me little about the city and virtually nothing about the boating in the area. I had only in the past year heard of that wonder of wonders, Shilshole Marina. My memories of Seattle largely dated from a birthday trip to that city when I was eight, and vaguely encompassed the train depot, the ferry terminal, and an incredible shower at the Olympic Hotel that had a dozen showerheads and a bench.

We carefully loaded our Super Beetle one Friday morning, and right after work we headed for the big time. It was with a feeling of excitement and suspense that we followed I-5 to an exit that somehow led us to the Ballard area, not far from Shilshole. Once there we were literally speechless. We trekked from one end of Shilshole to the other, gawking about us at the endless number of boats, and we still mustered vitality for Gove's Cove. This was sailboat heaven compared to the marinas of Portland. Our weekend came to an end just as we were beginning to scratch the surface of this boating paradise. Our return trip to Portland, and the weeks that ensued, contained little else but sailboat talk. We began to talk name brands and equipment like we ourselves were brokers. And we were now certain of one thing: the $10,000 liveaboard was nonexistent. We agreed that we might have to pay $20,000, or maybe even a little bit more. But $30,000 to $35,000 was out of the question, for a person could buy a whole house for that amount. But even as we said this we were both beginning to realize that $30,000 might be cheap.

Had we known boaters or liveaboards then, we might have saved ourselves a lot of legwork and expense in making our sojourns to Seattle. But we knew no one in boating, so we could only grope our way along. Could we have sat and talked with a friend with personal experience we might have saved ourselves considerable time. We had not even sailed on a big boat. It was very difficult to find what we were looking for because we really didn't know what it was we even needed. We read books. We read articles. We saved money. We kept returning to Seattle.

A break for us finally came at the Seattle Boat Show. We moved as if in a trance, patiently waiting in long lines to climb aboard one exquisite boat after another. We stood crowded in main cabins designed to accommodate at most six people with ten or twelve other dreamers like ourselves. We admired the spit and polish of the boats, the quaint little doors with latches, the miniscule cubicles for bathing. We walked around the King Dome in a stupor and finally climbed to a secluded seat to drink our cokes and eat hot dogs.

"Nobody'll come out and say how much they cost, Tom."

"I know." It was not much of an answer, but it was a reflection of the hopelessness I was beginning to feel. We knew from our already limited experience that most of these boats would be in the $45,000 to $100,000 category at least.

"How do people afford stuff like this?" We agreed there must be a lot of wealthy people in Seattle, for even in our income bracket, which was considered high by government tax standards, we could not begin to afford $100,000.

As the show began to thin out for the evening, Tom saw his quarry. One lone salesman was organizing his materials and setting up for the next day's onslaught. Like a warrior to the front lines, Tom marched over and began interrogating him. The sales representative had a captive audience, and perhaps his sales were down, for he dragged us to his warehouse, wrote figures down, scratched them off, refigured, rewrote, and rekindled our hope. We had finally gotten a ballpark figure from someone. It was not a boat we were interested in, but we'd gotten someone to commit to a price on a boat in our size range. We now had hope. Our goal was achievable.

Many weeks later, while we were again in Seattle half-heartedly investigating the possibility of a kit boat, and also looking for the umpteenth time at other boats, we saw it. We both knew instantly that the 34 foot boat was the end of our intense search the moment we climbed aboard.

We talked with the dealer at length and he informed us that he had an office in Portland and that should we be interested it would be easier to go through the Portland office. We had a ball park figure, a brochure, and a feeling in our hearts that this boat could be ours...the Cal 2-34. We still did not have a down payment, but at this point the couple of thousand more we needed seemed a minor matter. We spent the entire trip back to Portland deciding whether we'd replace the interior carpeting with teak or oak flooring, and how we could personalize the interior to fit our needs. We were momentarily relieved to have found a good boat in an "affordable" price range, but the next few months brought about a new tension in the drive to save the almighty dollar. To help us ascertain the exact amount we'd need for a down payment, a few weeks later we sought out the Cal 2-34 dealership in Portland.

Horror of horrors! As we drove into the parking lot we recognized the building as the one which housed our black haired antagonist that we'd months earlier sworn we'd never buy a boat from. We sat in the car in gloomy silence broken finally by Tom's question, "What do you want to do?"

"I don't know," I growled.

We sat there for some minutes reflecting on the humiliation we'd both experienced at the hands of this man some months earlier, and begrudgingly had to admit that he'd been right about the cost of boats.

"Well, we might as well go in. Maybe he won't remember us, and besides, think what idiots we used to be wandering around looking for a boat for $6,000." We both started laughing at our folly, and agreed that if we wanted the Cal we would have to go in. We had to know how much we needed for a down payment. We held our breath and entered.

FORWARD

PROGRESS

"WELL, WE'VE GOT ANOTHER PAYDAY coming up, plus we can have a garage sale and get rid of a few items," Tom suggested.

"Oh, God! Garage sales are stupid, Tom. We won't make any money at that!"

"What do you mean, Beck? Garage sales are a great way to make money."

"Fine. You have your garage sale. I'm not going to be bothered. I just can't believe you sometimes!" I reluctantly ran an ad in our local paper for Tom's garage sale, which I decided would be held on Wednesday evening from five to nine—hardly a propitious time for a sale, but those were the days in which I thought garage sales a total waste of time and effort.

Wednesday afternoon we came home from school and Tom set up his goods under the cover of the carport, since it was a rainy, nasty day. I curled up on the couch with a blanket and a good novel and chuckled at his folly. "Poor guy," I mused. "This'll make for a good laugh in years to come."

Thus assured, I read on and sometimes wondered if he wasn't getting cold just standing around outside waiting for his mysterious customers to appear.

17

About 6:00 the door opened and I sniggered from my prone position, "Whatsa' matter? You getting cold?" But Tom was oblivious to my taunts, for he was intently counting out a wad of bills he had withdrawn from his pocket. I listened in disbelief, but when he reached the $280 mark I shot off the couch and gasped, "Are you kidding me?" My eyes were popping out as I saw the bundle of bills, and I quickly began careening about our condominium, grabbing everything in sight, from old orthodontic retainers to vases and touristy ashtrays. I could not find things fast enough.

The customers quickly dropped off for the evening, however, but a new money-raising gimmick was now at my disposal: The Garage Sale. In such manner we quickly raised the balance needed for our down payment. It was spring break when we ordered our boat, and not a minute too soon, for shortly after that the base price shot up another $2,500, to be followed quickly by even greater increases!

The day we placed our order was probably one of the more eventful days of our young lives. The broker went through what seemed like pages of optional equipment we could choose from, including the color. But between the order and the arrival existed some ninety days, and much of our time in that interval was spent organizing garage sales. Our rented condominium became barer and barer. Our dinette set went, dressers went so quickly we realized we had not asked nearly enough. Skis, trap shooting gear, decoys, camping equipment, washer, dryer, clothes, college beer mugs, plants, and end tables flew out the door. Then one day our living room furniture disappeared. We now had what seemed like a vast condo with only a bed and kitchen utensils (I had sold our plates). And then, two months before our boat was due, our bed went.

"Good grief, Tom, now what are we going to do?"

Tom agreed that we had gotten ahead of ourselves, and so we sat on the floor of our now monstrous condo and deliberated for some hours. It was ridiculous to camp out in sleeping bags for two months on the floors of our rented apartment. It was then I thought of my friend Jody who owned an apartment building in Portland and maintained a guest apartment there. One phone call later and we had a new address. So, we moved into an already quite full fifth story apartment with our vanloads of remaining worldly possessions. I had not realized there was still quite so much junk as I surveyed the apartment's previously cramped front room now made utterly impassable with our boxes of strange leftover mementos, most of which eventually found their way to my mother's attic. Even my newly constructed worm farm and my adopted cat, Orphan Annie, were included in the shuffle. Anyway, in this headquarters we slept and ate, but the rest of our time was spent sailing our recently acquired garage sale El Toro on the Willamette River, much to the amusement, concern, and consternation of other boaters, and in seeking out moorage for our boat.

With literally nothing to do at home, we spent a lot of time searching for moorage for our new boat, and becoming dismayed over the lack of available moorage (and our dislike of what was available) when we got a tip from a friend who suggested we check with a Harold Parker on Sauvies Island.

In describing Harold it is impossible to do him justice. Kind is overused; gentle is sappy. But both are true. A bright eyed, energetic, slender man with a beautiful sense of humor is a general description of that character who was seeing the realization of a dream come true that he had entertained for years as he'd lain in a hospital bed recovering from a near fatal accident as a hard-hat diver. Harold had dreamed of having a moorage along his property where he could sit in the comfort of his farmhouse and watch the stately procession of beautiful sailboats glide by his window. And when we first met him in 1976 his dream was beginning to materialize.

His love and affection for nature and life were contagious. Once, uncovering a nest of newborn baby mice in his field, he could not bear to leave them to burn up in the hot sun, so he covered them with a wooden structure. "At least give 'em a chance," he explained to us. Another time, angry at the bird droppings all over the side of his house, he went to remove the nest, but when he found it full of babies he could not bring himself to destroy it, so he propped 2 x 4's all along under the eaves to catch the droppings until the birds could fly away. He was a gentle soul. He was our honorary commander-in-chief at the moorage. He was our father. Sometimes he was our child. I speak not just for my husband and myself, but for those first early residents at his unfinished moorage.

Thus assured of a slip at Harold's private marina, Tom and I felt comfortable in wandering out to Sauvies Island several times a week and hanging around the only partially completed docks, dreaming of the day when our boat would be gently rocking there. Harold would rib us about our anxiousness. We were, by the end of May, aching for our boat, dreaming of nothing but our boat, and talking of nothing else. How boring we must have been to our friends who patiently endured our endless blather.

At last, it arrived on June 21, 1976. So intensely had we waited that the actual arrival of the vessel was almost anticlimactic. Together we viewed our beautiful *Cabaret* for the first time. We sat in her; we adored her; we were enthralled, but we were utterly dismayed when we found out it would be at least two more weeks before we could take possession. Two weeks seemed like a prison sentence, but there was little we could do.

In the interim we decided it would be appropriate if we sent announcements to all our friends telling them of our happy addition. I could only find baby announcements, so I bought several packages that had a nautical theme and jokingly sent them off with the arrival date being June 21, 1976, length 34 feet, weight 10,000 pounds, and name *Cabaret*. It was several weeks later that I met a friend of mine that I found out the joke was on me.

"Becky!" Mickey began in great enthusiasm. "Congratulations!"

I dumbly stared back trying to figure out what the joke was going to be. "Congratulations for what?" I asked perplexed.

"Oh, come on! You know what for!" Again the look of surprise.

"Well," I was grabbing for possible ideas. "You mean on my passing my test?"

"Oh, Becky! Come on! For your baby!"

I'm sure my face must have been a study indeed. "Baby, Mickey?"

"Yes! *Cabaret!* What an unusual name!"

"Mickey, you saw me just a short time ago. Did I look pregnant? Am I that out of shape?"

"No. I even asked Elaine if you were pregnant and she said she didn't think so, so we figured you and Tom had adopted." Now Mickey was becoming confused.

"Mickey, did you happen to see you much that baby weighed?" I smirked.

"Yes! It was a big baby! Ten pounds, wasn't it?"

"Try 10,000 pounds, Mickey." I mouthed thousand very slowly and distinctly. "Mickey, that was our boat I sent you the card on."

We both had a good laugh, and Mickey admitted somewhat pink cheeked that she'd gotten the card at work and had been very busy so she'd only glanced at it before she'd put it in her desk drawer. I wondered how many other people had done the same.

"Well, I'm glad I didn't buy you a baby present yet!"

But the boat might as well have been our baby, for when we took possession on July 21, 1976, or I should say the day it took possession of us, our lives were never the same. We took the long trip from the broker's dock on the Columbia River, down the river to the Willamette, and up the Willamette to Multnomah Channel. I was so nervous going under the bridges that I went below every time we passed under one, for I could swear that the mast would not clear. We were so proud! And the bow seemed so FAR from the stern! The boat seemed more like 50 or 100 feet than 34.

In the two days that followed we hauled box after box from our van into the confines of *Cabaret*, and magically it all seemed to disappear without a trace. Not that the water line stayed the same, however, nor would we ever see it again!

We began to recognize immediately not only the joys, but the costs involved in owning a boat. Much of Tom's pay that summer went for electronics, a propane range and tank, shore power cord, and a myriad of very expensive little items, from bumpers to line to insulation to many many dollars worth of teak for a teak deck box and a forward hatch to our chain locker, which was still without an anchor, chain, and windlass, and was being used as a blouse and shirt closet for the time being. Our list of items to put on the boat grew dramatically:

150% genoa	radio direction finder
CQR anchor	kerosene lamps
Windlass	a boat heater of some type
100 feet of chain	wisker pole
sextant	radio receiver
barometer	self-steering vane
clock	mainsheet winch
chronometer	main halyard winch
an extra propane tank	jib halyard winch
extra stays	a boom tent
a dodger	sail covers
air vents	wheel cover

The list took several weeks to reach its full form, for we were neophytes in the world of "cruising" and had much yet to learn. Ultimately we found an Avon, 4 horse Johnson outboard motor, hard shell dinghy, autopilot, man-overboard pole, EPIRB, and hundreds of dollars worth of insulation also worked their way onto our list. Fortunately these things did not become apparent all at once or I'm sure we would have despaired.

But for that summer we treaded water and managed to keep everything paid. We figured we were in no big rush since we'd have twelve years of payments before we could really do much traveling, and life was so wonderful then that we didn't figure we could ask for too much more. So we proceeded with those items we thought to be essential and decided we'd prioritize the rest of our list and do what we could when we could.

At first I was terrified whenever Tom would suggest an alteration to the boat, for I thought of *Cabaret* as perfect, and the sound of his jigsaw cutting through *Cabaret's* interior or decks made me quiver in fear. But after every project I had to admit that the boat was more functional for us and looked better yet.

Our summer was not all spent in ripping and rearranging. We spent as much time as possible sailing in the Willamette and Columbia Rivers. In fact, we sailed the boat on average every two days that summer, according to the log. More often than not we were joined by family or friends, and *Cabaret* established early her reputation for hospitality.

We found our moorage a literal haven and took great pleasure in the companionship of the four other boats with whom we lived that summer: Helen and Elmer Olson on *Elysium*, Craig and Molly Hull on *Osprey*, John and Rachel Wolford on *Bagheera*, and Ben and Elaine Clark on *Gamboleer*. Swimming every day, basking in our glory of boat ownership and the beauty of our surroundings was more than just fabulous; it was totally fulfilling. We would sit out in our cockpit in the evenings and listen to the serenading of crickets, the sound of wild ducks quietly quacking a few feet away, see swan sailing through the air only a few feet above our mast, and we seemed so extraordinarily pleased and content. Our dreams were at hand.

"Just think, Tom, when I'm 40 we'll be retired! I mean, how many people can lay claim to that? And in the interim between then and now, look at the beautiful life we're having." Somehow this did not ring true with me, but I was trying to be a good salesman to myself. It was like I was trying to convince myself that I could tread water for twelve years. With the hindsight now of twenty-five years, I can say for certain that I have never been, nor could I ever be, that patient...and passive. (This, of course, was the dilemma we had with ocean passages.)

Tom would concur and our thoughts would drift about like the passing current until the evening chill would force us inside. Orphan Annie too seemed enchanted with her new home. She had made her peace with Harold's little Schnauzer, Heidi, and had adjusted to *Cabaret* and life aboard in nothing flat. Upon our moving aboard she had twitched her nose for a day or two smelling the almost forgotten aroma of nature, and then she was off, soon to return, to my screaming horror, with five fat dead mice...surely her thank you gift to us for her new home! I guess we'd failed to train her that she was supposed to keep mice off the boat—not bring them on.

It was toward the end of summer when we found ourselves with two weeks at our disposal before the advent of another school year, so with much ado and pomp, we left on our first real cruise outside the Portland area. With a fond farewell from our neighbors and a borrowed Evergreen Cruising Guide of the Columbia River, we made our way without mishap to Astoria, Oregon, some 90 miles west of Portland.

I really shouldn't say the trip was without its mishaps, for both Annie and I suffered deep humiliations upon our arrival. In my excitement and nervousness at docking at a different place, I did one of my spectacular leaps from the boat about a minute too soon with only half a minute's worth of line. One foot brushed the dock before the line became taut and I was jerked backwards.

"Let go!" Tom yelled. But I stubbornly clung to the line and was towed through the water while being beat up against the side of the boat. Were those two aching hollows my armpits? I saw sturgeon heads floating by my face and slicks of oil coated my clothes. "How thoughtful of you to put yourself as a bumper between the boat and the dock," Tom teased. I was so embarrassed I wanted to cry as I dragged my wet battered body onto the dock, especially when I heard a couple of fishermen snickering wildly while they pretended to gaze nonchalantly at a nearby piling. I went below with a burning lump in my throat. Naturally we ended up having to move the boat to another slip, but this time I docked and Tom nobly fended *Cabaret* off.

We were no sooner resituated, however, when Annie leapt ashore and headed for the smelliest fishing boat on our dock. She, too, failed to negotiate her leap, for the boat had a stainless steel shield over the side of it for dragging nets up and her claws could not grab hold. Down she went and completely disappeared in the water. Before

I could scream for help, she popped up and, in one surge, hit the dock and then the boat again. She crawled under a greasy engine box, and I had to climb aboard to retrieve her. Once aboard *Cabaret* she hid in the bow and pouted for several hours. Actually, we pouted together.

Aside from this initial disgrace, all went well, and we sailed almost every day for two weeks over the Columbia River Bar and into the mighty Pacific Ocean. The first day into the ocean I was so frightened I insisted on wearing a life jacket, and the swells seemed so monstrous I could not tell sometimes if we were going forward or backward. I burped and yawned a lot but held together otherwise. But the days when we sailed *Cabaret* in and out over that killer bar that could be like a lake were unforgettable. How marvelous it was to set sail and go on one tack for hours without making a single major adjustment or continuously having to tack to avoid sandbars, river tugs, barges and ships. Unfortunately, these days would forever spoil river sailing for us. (My twelve year pay-off retirement plan was tarnished already.) On our return home we even planned an overnight anchorage—our first ever—and though we were not equipped with a fraction of the ground tackle we would later carry, we pulled in behind Walker Island and dutifully set our bow and stern anchors according to Chapman and tried to relax. I know each of us checked out the porthole a dozen times that night to make sure the city of Longview was where it was supposed to be. It always was.

Labor Day again found us racing down river to Astoria for a weekend of salmon fishing, but we found the weather adverse, and we got our first real taste of why the Columbia River Bar is not to be taken lightly: what had taken us only an hour and a half to motor out over took us over six hours to come back against!

We took a third trip to Astoria over Christmas vacation, only this trip proved to be a learning experience of an unprecedented degree. Our return trip was our first experience with truly adverse conditions, and we found out how utterly unprepared we were. We left Astoria at 6:00 A.M. with the flood tide. It was pitch black out but we felt we needed the time in order to make the return all in one day, unlike our trip down. Tom was to get the boat underway and take the first watch so I could sleep in. We had no more than left the calm and quiet of the marina though than the boat began to pound and crash violently. I thought Tom must surely have taken a wrong turn and was heading for the ocean instead of the quiet passage up the river. The motion was so terrible I could not stand upright. Nothing was stowed properly, so items were flying about haphazardly with a tremendous crashing and uproar. I was afraid I would get sick so violent was the pitching of the boat. I was trying to get dressed when suddenly the hatch came flying open and a drenched Annie was hurled into the cabin. The cat was wild-eyed and huddled in the corner yowling in a most nerve wracking way. She had been caught in mid-air by Tom as she was being swept overboard. Finally I staggered outside to be hit by huge waves crashing over the bow.

"Are you headed the right way?" I yelled at the figure in the black night.

"Yes!" came back a muffled response as a stinging sheet of spray raced the length of the boat and shot into Tom's face.

"Oh, God, Tom! Do you think I should call the Coast Guard?" My heart was beating heavily, for the inky blackness and unexpected seven foot chop had unnerved me completely.

"No!" Again the icy stinging spray in the face. I slumped onto the seat and tried to spot buoys in the darkness that were all but impossible to recognize from the seas and the city lights of Astoria in the background.

The wind, an east one which always signifies freezing cold when it comes to the Northwest in the winter months, was blowing perhaps thirty knots and had kicked up a six to seven foot chop across the open area of Astoria Bay. *Cabaret* would cut through the first four or five waves, but then would fall before the next which would sweep the decks full length. I was beginning to see that the dodger Tom had talked about having installed and that I had balked at would be an excellent idea after all.

We continued like this clear to Puget Island before the seas dropped off. Relieved and frozen to the bone I went below to heat up some tea and a can of chili—the combination seemed perfect. I was shaking visibly, but the onset of daylight and the thought of something hot were having a tranquilizing effect. Oops! Were we out of propane? Of course it was our only tank because we had procrastinated buying the second one since there always seemed to be so many other items on our list that were more exciting than a spare propane tank! It was New Years Day, and I knew we'd never get it filled along the river that day. So now it was freezing outside and inside, literally, because we also had no heat source other than an electric space heater.

Things did get worse because we also ran out of water due to standing in the shower with all our raingear on with scalding hot water pouring over us trying to warm ourselves up after each forty-five minute watch, about the longest we could stand in the freezing cold. We entered Multnomah Channel in the dark despite our efforts to be back before nightfall, and we groped our way down the channel in a blinding snowstorm. We dared not stop en route because we had no heat, no water, and no propane. The snow was falling so heavily we could not look directly ahead—we could only glimpse ahead every few seconds; the rest of the time we tried to maneuver up the shallow channel by watching the shoreline. Finally, we saw the lights of Parker's moorage ahead after what seemed like an interminable trip through arctic hell. We blasted our horn for assistance to dock since there were quite a few inches of snow on the dock and I did not trust my shaking legs to disembark. That night we slept in the main cabin with our small space heater blasting at us, and I wondered if I'd ever be hot again. Both of us ached for several days from so many hours of cold strain.

The trip, nearly a disaster, had taught us much about our lack of preparedness. We'd learned some lessons we'd never forget! Lessons that served us well in Alaska.

WE SAY GOODBYE

As WINTER PASSED AND SPRING became apparent, work resumed on the boats at Parker's, and *Cabaret* was no exception. Spring found us waxing, and sanding, and preparing to leave the nest. No matter how idyllic our moorage was, or how picturesque, or how unique, we found we were never again happy with river sailing after our trips to the ocean. We had spent a lot of time during the winter discussing our situation and had debated at length over the wisdom of forfeiting jobs that we knew would give us the income to pay off our boat in eight years...maybe seven if we really saved. Seven years was not so long on the one hand, but just to sit it out and not be totally happy seemed to be so wasteful of what precious time we have on earth. (My creative number crunching had convinced me we could be free in a mere seven years, not twelve!)

So we resolved to leave Portland and move to the coast, Newport specifically, since we had friends there, good moorage was available at a reasonable price, and we would have plenty of opportunity for ocean sailing and for playing in Yaquina Bay. Newport had everything for us—except jobs—but we felt we could always get some kind of job doing something.

The last months of the school year saw us accumulating a windlass, a thirty-five pound CQR, one hundred feet of chain, hundreds of feet of line, a dodger, and a second propane tank. In addition, we installed a refrigeration system in our icebox, and we mounted winches on our cabin top to enable us to run everything from the cockpit. We also purchased a storm sail for those stormy days we'd be out sailing (which went unused for four years!) We installed a secondary fuel filter system and bought our charts. Finally we were ready for our first ocean passage and, like a good omen, shortly before we left Portland Tom received confirmation that he'd been hired by Lincoln County School District, so at least one of us would be employed for sure! Our decision seemed better by the minute.

We made our last Columbia River voyage on June 16, 1977. We knew we'd be seeing everyone at Sauvies Island on a regular basis when we'd come to Portland for yacht club meetings or for visits, so it was not a strained farewell that morning as we left our slip, not like some farewells we have known. We waited in Astoria for the arrival of friends of ours who wanted to make the trip to Newport with us, but while waiting we learned of a new peril we'd never before experienced: fog. Time and again the weather report came in with Newport having zero visibility; Newport with ¼ mile visibility, now zero again.

Paul and Janel Smud, long time friends of Tom's, arrived late in the evening of the 17th and the four of us debated possible courses of action. Paul's experience at sea, a vast amount more than ours, was the ultimate determining factor, for he had spent many years fishing with his dad along the Oregon coast and knew it intimately. "I think you should wait," was his sound advice and something neither of us wanted to hear. Partially, our haste stemmed from the fact that Tom was to start summer school at Oregon State University the following Monday, and partially our haste was due to the impatience with which we both seemed to tear through life, a fault we have tried to curb with only moderate success. The next day brought some encouragement, however, for visibility was supposed to increase, and the Coast Guard expected it to clear completely by evening. That was all we needed to hear.

My first "official" log entry:

June 18, 1977
Today Tom, Paul, Janel, Annie and I set off for Newport. We decided at the last minute to leave. Reports from Yaquina were not good—fog and no visibility. Two calls to Jody in

Newport, however, convinced us that we should try for it, for she wormed an advanced weather prediction out of the C.G. there that sounded better.

Excellent bar conditions. We left Astoria at 9:45 A.M. and crossed the bar at 11:15 A.M. There was no wind so we had to motor for five hours!

Raised sail at 5:00 P.M. and have good wind.

5:30 P.M. we are sailing 5.1 knots. We are off Tillamook Bar in 46 fathoms. Wind is N.W. at 15 knots. Barometer is 30.2. Course of 165. Swells 3 to 5 feet. One foot wind chop developing. 50/50 sky. Cat is sleeping soundly.

Had to lower sails around 1:00 A.M. due to wind dying down. Clear night with calm seas. We motored to Newport, arriving here around 5:00 A.M. 6/19/77. We crossed a very calm bar and motored our way to our new slip.

The trip took a total of 18 hours from Astoria Bar to Newport bar. Slow.

The cat is queasy about her new home—other than that everything looks okay.

Not exactly a professional entry, but fortunately we never needed to know exactly where we were when, so it sufficed.

We spent July and August sailing the Pacific Ocean as often as possible and having a fair amount of fortune at fishing also. Many weekends we anchored in Yaquina Bay with our commercial crab pot off the stern and our poles dangling in the water. It was a nice way to escape the carnival atmosphere that seemed to envelope the Embarcadero, where we were moored. Often we felt we were living in a fish bowl there with one tourist after another peering in our windows without even checking to see if the hatch was locked or not. We began to appreciate and understand the attitude of boaters we'd run across before we bought *Cabaret* who had looked upon "tourists" roaming the docks with dislike. We tried to remain patient and friendly, however, for it had not been so long ago that we ourselves had been "tourists" peering at boats, but often it was difficult to refrain from asking the peekers where they lived so we could go and peek in their frontroom window!

But Newport, despite the irritation of being peeked at, was a port that was (and still is) endless in its attraction for us. Not many people think of the Oregon coast as an ideal cruising ground, but for those who do venture up and down the coast, a stop in Newport is a must, for it is virtually a haven on the central coast. Unlike so many of the bars along the Oregon coast, Newport's bar is short and almost always negotiable except for the worst of weather. The jetties are often lined with fishermen who will return a waved greeting, and an early morning arrival will have the pleasure of seeing a parade of fishing vessels steaming out for their day on the Pacific grounds.

More often than not, the summer winds roar out of the northwest and have a reputation for howling the entire length of the coast, making passage northward against the choppy seas and blasting winds seem virtually impossible at times. For people in that predicament, Newport can most easily be reached by making a night passage or playing the Waiting Game for the days of lull. For those southbound, however, Newport's refuge after an often wild roller coaster ride is welcome. In approaching from the north at night, care must be taken to be sure and go south of the north jetty for entrance. We have seen our share of vessels that have turned north of the north jetty, mislead by the lights on the bridge spanning Yaquina Bay, thinking that the entrance was at hand only to find themselves in the surf in short order.

Once across the mouth of the jetties, the remainder of the trip to the bay is accomplished with ease. The trip will unfold a panorama of sights, smells and sounds, for the passage to the public docks takes one past the colorful bayfront where boats unload their cargoes at the back doors of half a dozen canneries. Public dock facilities in Newport provide easy access to a delightful stroll down the busy little street of Old Town Newport. Shops (too many nowadays) some great restaurants, and a fair share of bars populate both sides of this narrow, busy street, crammed to capacity during the summer tourist season. Farther up the bay lay the private docks of the Embarcadero where guest moorage can also be obtained. The bay itself provides excellent anchorage for those who prefer the privacy of swinging on a hook. South Beach Marina, a vast open marina on the right as one enters the bay, also provides transient moorage. Although a long walk or a long row is necessary to get to the bay front from South Beach, it is a pleasant trip and one which feels good after being confined to a boat. In any event, Newport can house the wandering soul, whether at dock or anchor, and offers a delight of entertainment and scenery.

Into this beautiful and glorious setting we found ourselves in 1977. Who could ask for more? We were an easy two hour trip by car from

Portland (okay, two and a half hours) where our families and friends were, but we had the luxury of the ocean with its seaweedy smell and forlorn fog horns sounding in the distance. I loved to wake up in the middle of the night, although I rarely did, and look out at the fog among the rigging of the silent vessels. The foghorn always made me feel somehow sad, yet so glad to be in my cozy berth snuggled up to the slumbering Tom beside me. I knew I would have felt comforted by the horn though were I groping my way into the bay, and in fact, there were several times when its sad, beckoning call, helped us find safe passage back to port.

So our year in Newport progressed. Our jobs in the neighboring community of Lincoln City were good. (It turned out that I also got hired at the same school that Tom did.) Our occasional weekend trips to Portland provided a lot of diversion and entertainment, and our weekends spent in Newport were enjoyed tremendously. Many times we found the weather too unaccommodating for ocean or bay sailing, so we would spend our weekends traipsing along the beach looking for lost treasure swept ashore, or for any flotsam. On Sundays we would walk from the Embarcadero along the full length of the bay front, past the Coast Guard station, and up the beach to a pancake house. Once there, appetites whetted by the brisk walk, we'd order a scrumptious breakfast along with three or four side orders. Afterwards, too full to retrace our long trek, we'd take a shortcut, buy a Sunday paper and lay around for several hours reading and philosophizing. In five years (had it down to five now) the boat would be ours if we kept to the course we were on. That meant saving over $500 a month, a substantial amount when you consider we were also making boat payments of $325 plus still trying to rig the boat with various items, eat, dress, and enjoy life too. My figuring said we'd then probably have to work a year for cruising funds. But we both found ourselves driven to distraction as we'd watch boats pull into Newport for fuel and water, or just for a rest. Always they were headed somewhere enticing: Mexico, Hawaii, Alaska, the San Juans. "Well, one of these days we'll be going too," I'd sigh as we'd amble down the streets on one of our daily walks. But already we were feeling frustrated. We had planned on spending our summer vacation in the San Juans that year, but it already seemed disheartening that we'd have so few weeks there and we'd have to return for Tom's early football coaching. Five years began to seem like an eternity.

In February we spent an evening with a fellow teacher who informed us that he was going to Alaska in the summer to fish, and that if things worked out right he'd just stay there. Tom and I instantly looked at each other over a foaming pitcher of beer and read each other's thoughts. We were enthralled by his plan, and that very night when we were finally alone we resolved that we would go to Alaska in the summer too, only we'd stay for sure. It seemed so easy a decision, and so perfect, and so obvious. Wasn't Alaska the land of the get-rich-quick because of the pipeline? And wasn't that exactly what we needed—an opportunity to get rich quick? Like a great burden had been lifted from our shoulders we felt exuberant over our decision to leave Newport. Though we really liked it there, the lure of adventure and change could not be denied. We were sure of success and began immediately to see "signs" or omens that our decision was a right one. We'd walk down the street and suddenly see so many cars with Alaska license plates. "A sign," I'd say, nodding my head in the direction of the automobile.

"A sign," Tom would say as we'd drive past a previously unseen billboard advertising Alaska Airlines.

"A sign," I'd say as we'd sip beer in Jody's tavern where, hanging on a wall, was a calendar from a bar in Ketchikan.

Of course, while we were jubilant about our new adventure, others did not take to our plan so excitedly. Fellow teachers were speechless, but our families were not, and one would have thought we were wayward children and not people approaching thirty. I'm sure Tom's parents must have felt deserted since they had just moved from Coquille to the Portland area to be closer to relatives. And I'm confident that my mom, then unfamiliar with the terrain of the Inside Passage, envisioned black tempests in the Gulf of Alaska accompanied by two hundred foot waves and igloos everywhere in sight. Our unconcern about exactly where we were going and when we'd actually arrive was an alien experience for parents who had never had the luxury, or the interest perhaps, of doing what we were doing. For their peace of mind we mapped out a tentative itinerary which we promptly ignored and lost. Apparently they sent mail to us at practically every stop, but we never thought about checking for any.

Our teaching associates were completely surprised at our decision not only to quit our jobs, but to leave education entirely, and they quizzed us at great length as to our motives and plans. We found that our leaving without any jobs or prospects for one was just incomprehensible and unacceptable to most people, so we told them we had a "situation" lined up for Tom, whatever that meant. This seemed to assuage most people, although it made us feel sheepish to have to fib about it, but we felt it was worth not having to listen to a barrage of doubts and unending "what if" questions.

Only our former live aboard neighbors from Sauvies Island seemed to be completely supportive and enthusiastic about our plan. So, resignations in, teaching materials given away, and desks cleaned out, we were off on the biggest adventure yet.

NORTH TO ALASKA—NORTH TO THE RUSSIAN ZONE

OFTEN PEOPLE ASK ME what was my favorite place in our travels, and I vacillate…was it Mexico or Alaska? Mexico or Alaska? Twenty-five years have passed, and I no longer hesitate: Alaska. So why did I love the archipelago of S.E. Alaska so? I cannot begin to tell you precisely. It was everything; it was nothing. It was the beginning of a new adventure. It was the new frontier—the last frontier. Anything was possible there. It is a certainty that now, decades later when we once again prepare for adventures on the high seas (and highways) Alaska remains atop my list of ports of call. Perhaps it is the "call of the wild".

Preparations for the trip actually began quite a few months before school was out. We ordered a 150% genoa right after the decision to leave was made, and we sold one car right off which paid for a sextant (it seemed important for the trip at the time) radio receiver, and a hard shelled dinghy. At the last minute we ordered an Avon also, for the trip from Newport to the Straits of Juan de Fuca would be our longest "passage" yet and it seemed appropriate that we have some sort of life-saving device. Looking back, with that great advantage of advanced hindsight, both Tom and I agree that the best thing to have done to have prepared for our trip north would have been to store our propane cook stove and install a diesel stove. But we had been told repeatedly, and erroneously, that the weather in S.E. Alaska was just like Seattle weather. Having come from the northwest we knew Seattle's weather was very similar to Portland's, and we'd had no major problems with condensation when we'd lived in Portland, so why would we have problems up north if the weather were the same?

Our trips to Portland became more frequent and more costly as we suddenly started thinking of more and more items we should have aboard. We had the Spare Parts Syndrome and found ourselves thinking along the lines that if one spare is good—two are better. We bought oil, air and fuel filters by the case, and we added five jerry cans to our repertoire of deck clutter.

Through all the preparing we found we talked about nothing else but Alaska until I tried to make one of my world famous rules that we could only talk about the trip one night a week. Otherwise, I reasoned, we would become miserable with anticipation. I had ordered a subscription to the Ketchikan newspaper, so we decided we would only talk about our trip when promising looking jobs appeared in the paper. Since very few "promising" jobs appeared my proclamation was a failure.

I went about singing Johnny Horton's famous song, "North to Alaska." Much to Tom's glee, however, I had the words wrong and insisted that the song went "North to Alaska, north to the Russian zone." Tom laughed his head off, and I laughed harder yet when he told me the words should be "North to Alaska, north the rush is on." I couldn't believe his stupidity and laughed so hard I had tears in my eyes. Finally we bet a month's worth of dinner dishes on it. I still can't believe I actually lost!

I learned to make bread, a task I never dreamed I could do but which became so easy that by the South Pacific I made up new recipes as I went along. I must admit that sometimes the bread defied description, and occasionally it could be used as a bludgeoning weapon, but generally it was very good. We bought charts, chart books, sprouts and jars, long underwear (we thought we were getting a little extreme at this point—little did we know!) We obtained a health certificate for Annie. We learned to cut each other's hair, for I couldn't imagine going to beauty shops while supposedly on a cruise. At first this task involved a great deal of fidgeting by the one getting the hair cut, but we both always turned out presentable, so as time passed we relaxed more while under the knife, sort to speak. One would have thought we were heading off around the world so thoroughly we prepared! Much to our later chagrin, two items we had been advised to buy that we ignored, were an outboard motor for the Avon and dinghy, and an autopilot of some sort. We felt these items were truly out of place on a "cruising" boat, but we changed our minds about that also a thousand miles later.

We left Newport on June 13, 1978, on the tail end of a sou'wester to avoid the northwest gales of the summer, for we had talked to too many people who had horrid stories about trying to pound north in those winds. One friend had taken six days to get to Tillamook Head, about 75 miles away! Finally, main ripped to shreds, he turned about and was back in Newport in six hours. He waited for a lull and tried again. Other friends had spent twelve hours trying to sail north and had not made even three miles, so they too turned about after taking a tiring pounding. We were in for a big surprise, however, when we found out how much fury was still left in the tail end of a sou'wester. As we headed for the normally easy bar in Newport we both took turns commenting on the unusual swell rolling in. We were so anxious and so excited about leaving, though, that we both refused to let good, common sense dictate our course of action. We kept heading out with conditions deteriorating rapidly. Finally we reached a point of no return where we could not turn *Cabaret* around; we were committed to leaving, and as I looked at the monstrous swells coursing their way along I felt tremendous fear in the pit of my stomach. I looked over at the north jetty and vaguely wondered if I could swim that far with all my raingear on. Should I jump now or wait until the boat started going down? I glanced nervously at Tom, and when I saw his white face I realized things were bad indeed, for I had never known him to be apprehensive on the boat. Somehow these conditions did not match the Coast Guard's description of twelve foot seas with twenty knot winds. Two huge shrimpers, straggling in from the sea, lay outside the bar allowing us plenty of room to try our escape before they attempted to maneuver their giant craft over the tumultuous entry. I sat stunned and silent at our danger and folly in leaving.

Once outside we were pushed up the coast at record speeds. At one point on top of a swell a gust hit *Cabaret* so hard it spun us 180 degrees. The seas were gigantic. In the troughs we had no wind;

at the peaks we were blasted. We knew we'd never be able to make headway back to the safety of Newport. We lowered our jib, turned *Cabaret* around, and hung on as we surfed our way up the Oregon coast under reefed main alone maintaining an average speed of eight knots. I started getting sick once some of my initial fear abated, and I continued to be ill steadily for the next sixteen hours as we coursed along. I looked with pity at our poor, quivering Annie and felt even worse. She huddled in a cockpit combing compartment wild-eyed and terror stricken. I couldn't bear to look astern, for each monster wave looked like it would be the one to break into the cockpit and drown us, but each time the mountainous seas reached us, *Cabaret* rose from the valley and the wave would pass under the stern without a splash. We were both ashen with fear, if a cat can look ashen. I finally reached the point in my sickness where I didn't care what happened. I decided I would go to bed, and if I died in my sleep— well, too bad. Without saying a word to Tom I slipped into the quarterberth and dropped into a deep sleep. Tom and Annie kept us going through the night. The cat, finally venturing to poke her nose out of the combing compartment, was quickly stuffed into the front of Tom's coat for added warmth and some sort of distraction to keep him awake. Somehow he managed through the long, cold, pitch black night to hand steer without stop while I slept like a dead person. The next morning I awoke refreshed and well. I took over the helm, but Tom was so exhausted he could not go to sleep.

The wind had all but died by this time, and the seas were quickly flattening out. By 7:30 A.M. one would never have known that only 24 hours before we had been hurtled up the coast. Now we chugged along quickly setting aside the rigors of the night before. By 11:15 A.M. a slight breeze out of the northwest had sprung up, and by 3:30 P.M. we were pounding and crashing into a nor'wester. We decided the sou'wester might have been the easier traveling after all! When we finally spotted the light on Tatoosh Island, marking the entrance to the Straits of Juan de Fuca, we became positively silly and found everything hysterically funny. We knew the ungodly pounding we were taking would soon end, although at times when we were reduced to two and three knots we wondered about that.

We anchored at Neah Bay that night after a 37 hour marathon run of 200 miles. Though our apparent speed up the Washington coast had been reduced due to the pounding, we still averaged seven knots from Destruction Island by staying in close to shore and catching a northbound current that numerous fishermen in Newport had advised us of. At last, the hook down, we went below and silently devoured a quart of peaches before we collapsed into bed. If just a 37 hour trip had exhausted us so much at our relatively young ages, how would we ever stand a twenty or thirty day trip?

We had learned three lessons: leaving when we did under conditions we were not prepared for had been incredibly foolish. Looking back now I can recognize that, on the one hand, it was not a mistake without some benefit, for sooner or later ocean voyagers will be forced into some heavy weather sailing. On the other hand, why seek out those experiences any sooner than you have to! We did find out how well our boat behaved in tough conditions though, and that knowledge gave us a lot of confidence on later occasions when we again were in bad conditions.

The second lesson was that our boat could handle a lot more than we could. The third lesson we could no longer ignore was that Annie was just not ordained to be a cruiser. Why she had stayed by us as long as she had still baffles me. She got sick every time we took her out on the boat—she'd even gotten sick a few times just sailing on the river, and she had taken to abandoning ship in Newport every time the engine started. We had had to lock her in the bow until we were away from the docks, adding even more to her trauma, I'm sure. We assured ourselves, and her, that the traveling would be easy from then on, but we both knew we'd have to find a home for her before we left Alaska for any blue water cruising.

We put aside our concerns for the time, for now began those glorious, fabulous days of really, truly cruising. For the first time since we'd bought our boat we were really traveling on it, not just sailing in circles. As we wound our way through the San Juans and the Canadian Gulf Islands, we were literally enchanted. Each stop seemed the best, beginning with Victoria where we tied right there in front of the Empress Hotel. So this was what it was all about.

We learned also what people meant when they referred to the hidden and unexpected hazards and costs of cruising. We suffered our first equipment casualty at Kulleet Bay where our brand new half inch gold braid anchor line snapped as we were setting anchor, thus burying our 35 pound CQR and 100 feet of chain in some 50 feet of water. We looked at each other momentarily appalled, too surprised to have the wits about us to check landmarks instantly. Tom quickly got out our 45 pound Danforth and new line and got us reanchored. In the interim I tried to refigure exactly where we'd been when the line had snapped. We were sick about our loss and unable to figure out why the line had just popped in half, since there seemed to be no fraying or chafing. We spent the rest of the day in the sweltering sun trying to locate the anchor and chain, but it was impossible to free dive to such depths. We rigged up a grapnel hook and rowed about for hours in the blistering sun hoping to snag the chain...we caught a lingcod instead. Depressed and disgusted we left the next day for Nanaimo to replace our lost equipment.

Time for another lesson. In Nanaimo we bought new chain and 5/8 line, but we were unable to locate a CQR anchor anywhere, so we telephoned Portland and asked Tom's parents to bring us one when they came to meet us at Westview. We hauled our new chain and line back to the boat via taxi and tried to file our loss where it belonged - out of the way for the summer. We both rationalized our loss by saying how fortunate we'd been that it had broken when it did and not at a crucial moment when anchored in a big storm. Our troubles were not over, however, for we discovered, when we next went to anchor, that the chain we'd bought in Canada would not stay on the wildcat when we went to winch it in. It kept jumping out. Aha! There are lots of different makes of chain, and 3/8 of one kind may not have the same measurement as 3/8 of another. So for the summer Tom got a daily workout hauling 100 feet of chain and a 35 pound Danforth in every time we moved. In the Canadian islands where anchorages are relatively shallow, there was no problem, but once the anchorages got deeper it proved to be a real fine workout for him.

In Nanaimo we learned what a great ambassador we had in Annie, for we met the first of many people there through her that I doubt we'd have met otherwise. One afternoon I looked out the companionway to see a towering, handsome woman cuddling Annie and carrying on a real conversation with her. I stepped into the cockpit to say hello and met Nancy Smalley of M/V Turtle from Friday Harbor. Nancy and her husband, Fred, were cat fanciers it turned out, and even though Annie was far from being a pedigreed feline, Nancy had been taken by Annie's friendly overtures. A sad fact was that our cat was not the aloof, independent type one usually thinks of when one thinks of cats; Annie would go to anyone, literally, and demanded almost constant attention, holding, petting, and cajoling...much to our distraction and annoyance at times. Nancy invited us over to meet her cat, Poppy, but since neither Tom nor I were real cat lovers (except for Annie) the idea of seeing someone's cat was not terribly enthralling, but I acted enthused because Nancy had been so friendly. Little did we know it then, but Nancy and Fred would cross paths with us many times for many years.

In fact, our second encounter with them was at Princess Louisa Inlet. We had had one of those rare treats in sailing where we had flown up Jervis Inlet under genoa alone and had hit nine knots with a few gusts. It had been an exhilarating day which would be topped off by spending three glorious days at the head of Princess Louisa. Immediately upon tying up, we jumped overboard—this was one of Tom's rituals during our travels, and he still regularly dives over the side no matter where we are! We crabbed off the docks in 300 feet of water and hauled in gigantic Dungeness. At first everyone eyed us skeptically, but once they saw the huge crab we laboriously dragged up from the bottom, other crab pots began going over. I caught a gigantic shark (okay, three foot) which scared me to death but brought out some hidden ichthyologists at the dock and they carefully analyzed it and identified parts for the onlooking crowd.

We hiked the trails and enjoyed the lush density of the woods until I began to worry about bears after Tom foolishly pointed out fresh bear sign to me. Annie, too, enjoyed Princess Louisa. In fact, we began to wonder if she might be considering changing her nationality to Canadian, for each morning we found fresh evidence in the cockpit that she had been ashore hunting. I awoke one morning to see a whole crowd of people standing by our boat staring very intently. I naturally was bursting with pride that so many people thought our boat so beautiful. When they started laughing, however, my beaming faded and I looked out into the cockpit to see that the now applauding onlookers were watching Annie play with an abducted mouse. When the mouse finally made a suicide plunge off the stern the crowd dispersed and Annie skulked into the cabin for her day long nap.

We left Princess Louisa a week later and headed for Westview where we were to meet Tom's parents. We had bought ourselves anniversary presents there a few weeks early. I bought Tom a spear for diving, and he bought me a snorkel and fins, my first ever. These presents were probably the best we've ever bought each other, for they opened a whole new world of activity. I cannot begin to recount the hundreds of meals we have had that Tom has speared.

In the weeks that followed I spent hours flapping away in the water staring fascinatedly at objects. Always I was looking for some ancient Egyptian artifacts that would be worth a fortune. I found instead lots of pretty rocks and shells. The first time Tom went diving with his new spear I figured we'd be eating canned meat or something similar that night, for I never expected him to spear any fish until his third or fourth day since it seemed like a pretty tricky thing to do. On his third dive, up popped a grinning face followed by a three pronged spear with a big rock cod securely stuck.

We spent two weeks in July shuttling parents in and out of Westview. Tom's parents arrived first, with our new CQR, and spent a week enjoying the delights of Desolation Sound. My mother came next, but stayed in a motel...not on the boat. She would build up her stamina for that by Mexico, however. Finally, the 21st of July we turned the boat north and headed once again for the warm waters and beautiful islands of Desolation Sound. The weather turned hot and more than ever we enjoyed the lazy days at anchor in Prideaux Haven. Our typical day consisted of getting up to a monstrous breakfast of pancakes and glasses of juice; this would be followed by a hike in search of lost lakes or abandoned treasure. This exertion would last only as long as we could stand the hot, sticky, mosquito-ridden woods. We would then return for an afternoon of snorkeling and dawdling, to be capped off by a dinner of freshly speared fish and tasty, just shucked oysters from the rocks. This was the finest of living, and our memories of Prideaux Haven teased us often during the cold, rainy months in the Alaskan north.

Annie, too, settled into a routine—not exactly one that we would have chosen for her, however. Her day was spent snoozing in any shade available. She learned almost immediately, however, that the clicking of the fishing pole's reel was worth her while to investigate, nap or no. She became an avid fishercat and greedily pawed at anything we brought up. She even stooped to swiping bait from the bucket! Nevertheless, it was not until the sun set that Annie would emerge in her full glory. Her first act, invariably, would be to check out the bow to make sure we were, in fact, anchored and hadn't moored to a dock during one of her naps. She would sit there staring vacantly at the passing water and other obstacles for a long time—just about until our bed time! Then she would begin her exercise routine and gallop heavily up and down the deck, dash out onto the boom tent we often set up for extra shade, and scrabble about on it making as much commotion as possible. After several hours of listening and fretting about her falling overboard I would finally drop off to sleep. Only Annie knows what she did in those quiet, dark hours alone. Every morning she was still aboard, though, ready to fish…and sleep away another day.

One morning we awoke to the realization that the summer was moving on, but we weren't. We had come only a small portion of the trip with hundreds of miles still ahead and most of the summer behind. With great reluctance we said farewell to the Smalleys and left what surely must be the most excellent boating along the entire Inside Passage. One day north of Desolation Sound the water became too cold for swimming and we had to put an extra blanket on our bed. Out came the kerosene heater the Smalleys had insisted we take with us, and out also came sweaters and hats.

We encountered a whole new experience from Stuart Island north, and that was the "Era of Rapids Running". We had previously negotiated Dodd's Narrows and Malibu Rapids into Princess Louisa, but now came a series of rapids with reports of whirlpools, five foot overfalls, and tales of 15 knot currents. Needless to say I was quite nervous about the obstacles facing us, so we attempted to plot a course that would avoid the biggies, like Seymour, Surge, Hole in the Wall, and Okisollo. We opted instead for a series of smaller rapids whose ferocity could be maneuvered against in most cases. In due time, however, we would end up going through every rapid in the area save for Arran Rapids which we had heard is so tumultuous that on large tides, a 25 foot overfall sweeps through, pulling bottom fish from the bottom and churning them upwards where they fall prey to awaiting eagles. How much of this is fact and how much is lore I will leave to another more adventurous than I to discover.

Though the weather continued fair, we found we did not lollygag at anchorages once swimming was eliminated, so in short order we arrived at Port Hardy and prepared for the Queen Charlotte crossing and the second leg of the trip through Canada. We had heard a great deal about the fog in the Queen Charlottes, and we were not to be disappointed. The morning we left our anchorage at Port Alexander visibility was good although we could see a fog bank way out. "It'll probably burn off," we assured each other, but we took the precaution of plotting courses and estimated arrival times a little more carefully than usual. It was a good thing, for barely had we cleared Browning Passage than the fog socked in so thick we could hardly see the bow of the boat. One of us stood forward ringing a fog bell with fog dripping off our eyelashes while the other literally had to stare at the compass to maintain course. We were to make a course change at Pine Island where there was a fog horn. Steadily we advanced until we heard the horn regularly bleating. It seemed so close we felt like we could reach out and touch it, but we could not see the thing that was now blasting at the side of the boat. We changed course and, in due time, the fog lifted and we happily were where we were supposed to be. Two years later on a return trip we passed by this horn within a half mile, but in the heavy overcast we could not hear it. A look at the rocky shoreline and remembering how loudly the horn had blasted gave me shivers.

The further north we headed the fewer boats we saw, but every chance we got we questioned people who were heading south or whose boat had an Alaskan hailing port. Most people expressed concern that we were heading north so late in the season. Late? It was still August, and August was a nice month in Puget Sound, so why would it be late in the season for S.E. Alaska? We also began receiving discouraging reports as to the abundance of high paying jobs...and in some cases the total lack of jobs. Oh dear. We looked at each other in dismay and for the first time began to consider the possibility that maybe we'd been too hasty in our decision to leave our good teaching jobs. One fellow explained to us that we should be settled in somewhere by September, for once the fishing season faded a lot of fishermen took jobs ashore. "Plus," he advised, "the weather can start turning as early as September. It's hard to say."

We were speechless. What about the Indian summers of the northwest? Beautiful days of 80 degree weather. "If nothing else, Tom, at least we'll have had a nice cruise and gotten to see Alaska," I pointed out. We couldn't back out now, and besides, maybe things weren't as bad as everyone intimated.

So, with these concerns in mind we inched our way across the charts and steadily made progress. Stops at Pruth Bay, Namu, and Butedale provided helpful distractions for us. Butedale was Tom and Annie's favorite stop. It was an abandoned town, still intact, with only a caretaker and his family in residence. The town, however, was perpetually lit up because the waterfalls there produced so much electricity that if they shut the lights off the turbine would burn up, or they'd blow a fuse, or something serious along those lines. The old hotel had showers with unlimited hot water. It was like going through an old-West ghost town. You could see where the café had been, peek into abandoned houses, poke about in the old hotel, and try to picture the person who'd had this room, or the waitress who'd served coffee in the tiny café. I have since heard that the town has been purchased.

Annie had to be hunted up and dragged out from under the old cannery buildings twice, which resulted in her being locked on board until we left. That she was tiring of traveling was becoming obvious, and we regretted again our decision to haul her around with us.

We now had sporadic weather. A nice day or two were followed by several days of low clouds, drizzle, rain, and fog. We had a southerly sweep through and it gave us several days of excellent sailing with headsail alone. Despite the weather, or maybe because of it, there was a quiet beauty in the northern landscape that was intoxicating.

We were getting anxious to get to Alaska. The closer we got, the more restless we became, so it was with some impatience that we navigated through Grenville channel and finally into Prince Rupert. Here again we almost lost Annie, this time to a fisherman's gillnet. We awoke one morning to the knocking of a fellow traveler telling us that our cat was caught in some nets at the end of the dock. I found a shivering, wet Annie, mewing anxiously while she was literally trussed up like a bandit. She had shoved her head through three or four net spaces and had then tried to back out. In the process she got two legs strung up and was half choking to death. I panicked when I saw her predicament and was petrified that she would be strangled right before my eyes. As we tried to maneuver her head out of the noose-like net, she kept shoving it toward us, purring loudly, in gratitude I guess. I left Tom with her while I charged back to get a knife to try to cut her loose.

"You can't just cut up the guy's net, Becky!"

"Oh yes I can! We'll just pay him for the net, but she's being killed in there!" I dashed off with raincoat flapping, fuming that we'd brought her on this trip. Fortunately, when I got back with the knife Tom had already freed her and she hightailed it for the boat to gobble some food and water. "Well, I bet she never goes near a fishing net again!"

We left Prince Rupert for our long awaited destination: Alaska. It was fitting that the weather was beautiful, for it was a wonderful welcome to the land we'd both dreamed of seeing. We could only guestimate when we crossed the U.S.—Canadian Border, but we probably were not more than a few minutes off. Alaska. We were so wild with excitement we broke out bottles of long cherished beer (the B.C. Brewers had been on strike that summer) and we drank toasts to everything from Alaska to Prideaux Haven, to Oregon, to the Old Man in the Sea. It was an afternoon of big grins and joyous whoops. It seemed like a day of triumph.

That night we anchored in Custom House Cove, and in the morning I went bezerk again and ran around the deck naked to celebrate our arrival. I'm not exactly sure what nakedness had to do with it, but it seemed a gesture of some extremity for me. Halfway around I suddenly felt very embarrassed and foolish, especially when I saw Tom looking at me like I was nuts. But I had to complete the lap now. I wondered how many people hiding in the Alaskan wild were watching me!

And so, we arrived in the Land of the Midnight Sun!

It Was the Best of Times...Our First Winter

W E ARRIVED IN KETCHIKAN on a blue-skyed, gorgeous day—the kind of day that can make any place look pretty. We slowly motored up Tongass Narrows and gawked at everything we saw. When we docked at Bar Harbor I could not help but stare raptly at everybody. These were Alaskans! And I studied them closely looking for their hidden magic. I saw right off that Alaskans are mighty fond of dogs, for the docks seemed to be rampant with them—big ones, too.

We located customs, and having once been cleared we set off to see this border frontier town. We were amazed at the number of automobiles for such a small city. "Eighteen thousand cars for nine thousand people to drive at full throttle on twenty-seven miles of road," Tom mused.

"I wonder why everybody is in such a hurry?" I asked. "I mean, where is there to go?" Neither of us could figure this out until we realized how many bars and liquor stores the town had.

"Of course," Tom concluded, "they have to drive that fast to make sure they make it to all the bars!"

I laughed, but more than once we saw people stagger out the door of one bar, hail a taxi, and ride three doors down to another bar.

Neither of us was particularly enraptured with the idea of spending the winter in Ketchikan. The moorage left a lot to be desired, and after seeing the town on a rainy day it did not seem quite so enchanting. Tom was convinced it was not the place for him when he heard how much the annual rainfall in Ketchikan was: some 150 inches a year! So after a few days of walking the colorful, narrow streets of Ketchikan we left for our next destination—Wrangell.

We headed up Clarence Strait on a sunny, windless day and marveled at the beauty of the area. Tom remarked how stunted the trees looked compared to the ones further south. I could not get over how isolated and empty the area was. It was nothing like the areas we had come from where boaters were always in abundance. We liked the privacy and solitude of travel in the northern reaches, and of course the beautiful weather gave us a perspective on the surroundings that was probably way out of proportion..

That afternoon we stopped at a little hamlet called Meyers Chuck and again found ourselves literally slack jawed with wonder. To begin with, our entry was one of the most startling experiences we'd ever had. As we slowly advanced to the rock-encased opening I went forward to look for submerged rocks, when suddenly I saw what looked like two gigantic football fields surface about 100 yards dead ahead. I stared in disbelief, but when the football fields surfaced a second time, closer yet, I grasped their true identity. Like a stricken person I staggered to the cockpit flailing my arms wildly and squeaking, "Whales! Whales!" through a dry throat. Tom immediately turned the boat hard over and slowed down. Calamity was not averted, however, for the whales too had altered course to avert us, so we were on another collision course. Up again rose the mammoth leviathans and, to our terror, they were again aimed directly at *Cabaret*. Tom furiously whipped the wheel hard over the other direction as I stood there gaping in paralyzed suspense. Again the whales surfaced, this time within two feet of our beam. Tom was able to see the barnacles on their backs in minute detail and could easily have reached over to pet one—had he been so inclined. Shaking in disbelief I had groped madly for the camera and of course missed everything. Fortunately we entered the bay to Meyers Chuck without further incident.

"This place is really primitive, Tom," I whispered as we entered the minuscule harbor. There were several very rustic cabins, smoke coming from the chimneys of a few of them, all connected by little trails hewn out of dense brush. A handful of dilapidated docks hung on to their pilings somehow, and we gingerly tied on to them, careful lest any sudden movements break the whole structure down.

It was difficult to estimate the population, for we figured some people must be out fishing as there was certainly no other "Industry" in town. Later we would meet the delightful "mayor" of Meyers Chuck, Steve Peavey, and even he was hard put to give us an exact population. "Oh, fifty give or take," he'd say in his Irish lilt. In our travels in S.E. we would see areas even smaller than this, but I suppose the memory of Meyers Chuck stays with us the most because it was our first exposure to such subsistence. In talking with other travelers one need only ask if they've been to Meyers Chuck. If an affirmative answer is given, a passing shadow of disbelief temporarily fogs the traveler's eyes, and no more about it needs to be said. Just having been there is enough.

The next day we left for Wrangell under sunny skies. I have often wondered if we had first seen Wrangell in pouring rain if we'd have been quite so taken with it. Probably not. Approaching Wrangell from the sea is like approaching a magic island. Set at the mouth of the Stikine River, it seems to nestle at the foot of the snow capped mountains on the mainland behind it. We studied Wrangell for some time through binoculars as we approached, for the town can be seen from miles and miles away. We could see virtually no movement. "I wonder if the place is deserted? I don't see any cars or people or anything, Tom."

Then Tom would look through the binoculars for awhile.

"Oh, wait! A plume of smoke. Must be a mill there and everybody's at work."

Still not having seen a soul, we entered Wrangell's harbor and headed for the fuel dock, hoping it would not be deserted also. "I kind of like this place," Tom murmured. I looked at him like he was nuts.

A blonde man stepped out, and as we filled our tank and jerry cans I commented to him, "Gee, this place seems pretty quiet."

"You think it's quiet now you ought to see it in the winter," he answered.

"Oh, yeah?" I found it hard not to appear surprised, for I couldn't then imagine any place, other than a morgue, to be much quieter. "What do people do here in the winter?"

"Nuthin'."

"That's interesting." Well, a man of few words, I thought.

We tied to the transient dock and took off up the dusty little street that led to the main part of town. The streets were deserted in the early evening hours, and we were enthralled by the prevailing quiet. It was such a dramatic change from the downtown of anywhere else at that hour that we could scarcely believe it. We walked the length of the town some three or four times laughing and talking quietly, for it seemed out of line to make any sudden loud noises or movements. We were truly amazed. The town looked like it was straight out of the old West. The buildings all had western style facades on them, and I kept expecting Gary Cooper or James Arness to step out and draw his weapon (several weapons were drawn and fired during our stay!). Again, Tom said, "You know, I really like it here, Becky. I could see spending a winter here."

I was beginning secretly to agree with him, but I wondered if he'd really considered all the ramifications of living here. "Tom," I began, "are you sure you wouldn't get bored here? Besides, I doubt there will be jobs here."

"I wouldn't get bored," Tom assured me, "but what about you?"

The next morning Tom visited the local boat shop and was even more convinced that Wrangell was for him. After having taught small boat building and construction classes for several years, Tom was ready to venture into bigger vessels. The owner happened to be on vacation, but the head shipwright said things looked promising, and to check back in two weeks when the owner returned. I couldn't get too enthused about looking for jobs for myself, for at this point the important factor was for Tom to get on in a boatyard, so it didn't really matter if I got a job or not until we knew for sure that he'd be hired. So we sat in our cockpit a second evening and marveled at the beauty of the weather in S.E. Alaska and the incredibly friendly people we'd encountered all day long. At first we thought people were mistaking us for someone else, but as the day wore on we realized that the people were just plain friendly. It was a novel experience, but we found out it was typical of Wrangell. The town's friendliness was one of its best assets.

Despite our intrigue with the small, island town, we decided we should definitely visit Petersburg and Juneau, however, for there was always the possibility that Tom would not get hired at the Wrangell boatyard, and perhaps Petersburg and Juneau would be even better yet. We doubted the latter, but we had two weeks to kill , so we left on the tide.

The forty mile trip to Petersburg was as beautiful as everything else had been, and the twenty mile trip through the Wrangell Narrows was fascinating. The best way, we found, to handle the narrows is to enter with the flood approximately two hours before slack water (depending on the speed of your boat, of course). The narrows flood from both ends, so if you can be halfway by slack water the current will have assisted you going in and then will assist you going out as the water ebbs both directions from the middle. The channel is clearly marked, and there are no dangers...except for passing ships and ferries in the very narrow passages. Many sailboaters we met over the course of two years were reluctant to go through the Narrows, but the trip is easy if you keep the tides working for you. The current will run savagely on big tides, however, so even if you have a boat with a lot of power, it is wise to watch the tides. Fishermen have told us of coming through the narrows when buoys layed over and were buried under the rushing water.

Petersburg, a beautiful little Norwegian town with a small mill, was a busy little place (compared to sleepy Wrangell). It too had a boatyard, but the yard did not capture Tom's imagination the way Wrangell's had. Petersburg did, however, have endless job possibilities for me, and the town had a movie theater! a swimming pool! and a tennis court of sorts. Moorage was available, although not quite as private as Wrangell's, and Tom was guaranteed a job upon the shipyard owner's return, but we could not shake Wrangell from our minds.

"Well, we've got time, Tom, let's go on to Juneau." And so the approach of September found us scooting up Stephen's Passage, dressed in long underwear, sweaters, hats and coats, dodging whales and icebergs.

"Tom," I questioned one day as though suddenly enlightened with a mind rending revelation, "have you ever seen icebergs in Puget Sound in August?"

"Hmmm....no."

I paused for a bit to let my slowly dawning realization hit with even more dramatic impact. "Tom," I said with controlled suspense, "do you know anyone who goes out boating in full, long underwear in Puget Sound in August?"

A momentary hesitation, then,"No."

"Tom, if the summers are this different, then what the hell are the winters going to be like?"

We looked at each other and laughed nervously. "Well, we'll see soon enough I guess." This led to several hours of speculation in which we finally decided that it would be okay with us if it snowed for, after all, this was Alaska.

"Good thing we got that extra heater from Fred and Nancy is all I can say!" How little we knew then.

After a night at Hobart Bay we left early in the morning to try and beat the wind blowing on our nose. The sunrise was spectacular coming over snow-capped mountains and green landscapes. We had to keep a close eye out for submerged whales sleeping just below the water's surface, and I tried to send out good vibrations so one wouldn't decide to ram us. I had just read *Survive the Savage Sea*, and I didn't want to be living a sequel to it, *Survive the Icy Iceberg*.

Juneau was the biggest shock to us of all, for it was a full fledged city, complete with freeways and buildings with elevators. We sent everyone a postcard of the Red Dog Saloon and we visited Mendenhall Glacier and the museum. We tramped up and down about the town, but we knew Juneau was not for us. "Heck, if I'd a wanted to live in a modern city I'd just as soon stayed down south," I commented to Tom. There were other problems involved with making Juneau our new home: there was no boatyard, a car would almost be mandatory, and most importantly, there was no moorage...hardly a minor detail.

With time running out, we chose to bypass Sitka and choose between Wrangell and Petersburg. Each had its benefits. One minute I favored one, the next minute the other. Only Tom maintained a staunch faith in Wrangell, but in actuality the decision was somewhat out of our hands, for we were dependent on Tom being hired. Our travels had taught us that Wrangell's boatyard was the more popular of the two, for we had heard it repeatedly praised as a boatyard of long standing reputation. It finally got down to considering the real basics, and we drew up a list of pro's and con's about each town, but it was an exercise in futility, for when all was said and done we were both basically more interested in Wrangell.

The owner was due back from his vacation any day, so we did not tarry as long as we'd have liked at Taku Harbor where we got our first king crab when a fisherman handed us each one out of his crab-pot when he saw us oohing and aahing and taking pictures. He also told us there were lots of raspberries on shore waiting to be picked, so we got a small bucket full and feasted on king crab and fresh raspberry cobbler that night. We left the next day though, for we both kept picturing hundreds of fishermen swarming the boatyard pleading for jobs when their fishing season ended. A steady stream of "What if's" kept plaguing me, but since Tom could not answer them any better than I could, I kept my doubts and worries to myself mostly and figured if worse came to worse we could go back to Ketchikan. "But I refuse to go back south this fall, Tom. Everybody would know we'd failed!" Then I would set about imagining scenes of people smirking and telling us they'd told us so.

"We won't go back, Becky. Everything will be fine."

Finally Wrangell came into view and we were again tied to the docks. I was a nervous wreck the next morning when Tom headed over to Hansen's Boatyard, and I kept adding things for him to be sure and tell Olaf, the owner. "Don't forget to be sure and tell him about knowing how to weld and that you've taught construction and built small boats and stuff, " I said for the hundredth time.

In fifteen minutes Tom returned and I anxiously read his face for a clue. It didn't look good. "Well, what did he say?"

"He said he didn't know. He said he just got back from vacation and didn't know what his needs would be and to check back tomorrow."

Over and over I questioned Tom trying to glean any tiny new piece of conversation in which I could find an omen. Tom is not a good one for repeating conversations verbatim, with details of facial expression and body language though, so I could elicit nothing hopeful or suggestive in his retelling of his interview. A long groan finally indicated the conversation was growing old for him, so I had to wait impatiently for the next morning to learn our fate. Again he returned quickly. A bad sign, I thought. He finally could keep a straight face no longer. "I start on Monday, eight hours a day, six days a week, time and a half on Saturday."

So Wrangell would be our new home! We spent the afternoon arranging for a slip, a post office box, opening banking accounts, and looking over potential job prospects for me, an unpromising situation. The telephone company was willing to install phone lines to our boat, however, so we had a phone installed and I registered as a substitute teacher. Thus, we became residents. We were quite ready to quit traveling for a time. The latter part of our journey had consisted of some very long days to make up time for the weeks we had spent laying idly at anchor, and an increasing tension had grown due to the uncertainty of our future income. We could get by on Tom's salary if we lived frugally, and what with my earnings we would at least break even on our venture, but the heady idea of striking it rich had faded to an embarrassing remembrance.

The beautiful weather we had experienced since our arrival in S.E. quickly passed, and the monsoon season of October began. We had always believed that the Oregon Coast was perhaps the rainiest place in the world until we saw the rains of winter in Wrangell. Overnight, large skiffs in the harbor filled with rainwater. We would walk along the docks and see the bows of small boats sticking up, held secure only by the strained mooring lines. It was incredible, and still it rained. We quickly acquired Alaska tennies (high topped rubber boots) and we watched the steady downpour in awe. Could there possibly be this much rain in the world? Surely the rest of the world must be having a drought.

November 7th the rains ceased and it began to snow. Tom and I were like little kids and hoped fervently that it would stay for awhile. It did! With the change in weather my waning spirits came around, for I had become restless and gloomy in the previous weeks, and no matter what kind of good things I'd tried to tell myself about how lucky I was to be in Alaska and having this wonderful experience (and blah blah blah) I had remained depressed. I finally realized that all my life I'd wanted spare time to do things I never seemed to have enough time for, so I began my "Home Study Improvement Courses." Each day that I did not get a call to substitute, I began my studies: for one hour I practiced shorthand...something I never mastered; for an hour I reviewed my Spanish and Portuguese; for the third hour I read philosophy. I even took a correspondence course in electronics. I could never understand how I could get all A's on the tests, but when I took our tape player apart to repair it, I didn't have the slightest idea what I was looking at. I ended up burying my fist in it in a fit of anger when I couldn't get it put back together and found extra parts laying on the table. Tom came home, took one look at the pile of parts on the table, one look at my face, and debated whether it was safe to enter the boat or not. To add insult to the whole situation, he somehow put the player back together...and it worked. Anyway, I took a long walk every day, and in the afternoons I worked on making Christmas gifts—it would be the "Year of the Latch Hooked Rug". The days passed more pleasantly for me. Soon I expanded my projects and spent a couple of hours several afternoons a week visiting residents at Wrangell's long term care facility. And magically the snow stayed! We were enchanted by the winter wonderland effect the white beauty of the snow performed on Wrangell. We were used to northwest winters where snow is infrequent and usually turns to ice and slush within a short while. The snow coated everything here and transformed the muddy, gray, little town into a new place. In a siege of enthusiasm, we ordered cross country skis from the local Sears catalogue store and rationalized our splurge by telling ourselves that at least we wouldn't have to pay for lift tickets. It was a wise investment, and we got our money's worth out of them that very winter.

We spent Thanksgiving aboard and I cooked a small turkey on the boat (a very small turkey with a broken chest that Tom had to smash in order to fit it in our oven) and we gave thanks that things were turning out so well. We had been incredibly lucky, for Wrangell was sewed up in the winter, and had Tom not been hired when he was we'd have probably not stood a chance of finding work in such a small town. For a refreshing change our conversation was no longer dominated by school goings on and students. We could both come home and leave our concerns at the companionway. We both no longer lived just for the weekend. We liked all the days of the week.

On Tom's days off each week we did things together, mostly exploring in my pirated skiff, aptly named "Pirate". The skiff had been holed and beached, and upon inquiring about it from a man I saw studying it one day I was told I could have the thing as far as he was concerned. Tom and I had gleefully hauled it away, and $35 later we had its body puttied back together and painted. I had bought a small outboard 4-horse Johnson motor earlier that fall as a belated birthday present for Tom, for we had found in our travels that sometimes some things were just too damn far to row to, and too dangerous to take the big boat in to. Outfitted with our 4-horse Johnson we would head out in our 14 foot aluminum skiff, albeit rather slowly, and poke about.

We would ski around town now after dinner, going over what we would in the spring find out were people's fences, staircases, gardens, and garbage cans. The streets were, of course, deserted, and we would glide along breathing in the clean, cold air and looking for likely objects to ski over. We could not get over being at sea level and having so much snow.

And now the weather grew so cold the harbor began to freeze over. Pumps froze, bilge lines froze, the bed even froze. Nightly as we'd crawl into bed I'd see a line of ice slowly building along the hull by the mattress. Some nights the sheets would be frozen to the line of ice, and I'd have to jerk them free. It slowly and continually grew, and I studied the encroaching ice each night, vaguely wondering what to do about it.

"Tom, what do you think will happen when this ice melts? Where will it go?"

"I don't know."

"Will it run down to the bilge, do you think?"

"Yeah. Probably."

I watched nightly. One day I discovered a thick layer of frost behind the cushions of the dinette. This discovery was followed by finding a sheet of ice on the hull under the bathroom sink. Even the bathroom cupboards were iced up. We ran a space heater and Fred and Nancy's kerosene heater full time and still we were icing up. We ran another space heater in the engine room along with a heat lamp. Everywhere ice and frost was creeping in. The boat was a mess! Would it ever be dry again? One day we managed to get our frozen mooring lines loose to go over to the fuel dock for water since their large lines were still running. I kept thinking the wheel was locked when I was trying to steer, but the steering cables were frozen. The fifteen minutes we were at the fuel dock without heat was all it took to freeze the hot water lines that ran from the hot water heater in the lazarette to the sinks.

I found out what would happen to all the ice, incidentally, when I awoke one night feeling clammy. I looked over to see steam rising from Tom. I cautiously felt about me and found the bed soaking wet. Mattress, sheets, wool blankets and pillows were sopping from the melted ice along the hull. We got up and dragged out our sleeping bags and finished the night sleeping in the main cabin. The weather had finally broken.

We spent a week in March slipping and sliding about icy, slushy streets, but the snow and ice disappeared rapidly, and soon only small, stubborn patches remained here and there in the shadow of overhanging eaves. We'd made it through the winter! We never thought we'd be tired of snow, but we were glad to see it go and the hint of spring appear.

April brought us three weeks of 65–70 degree weather and news that my mother was coming to visit in May. Little did we know that the superb weather we were experiencing was not only highly unusual, but was a precursor of a wet, wet summer. "When you get weather this good this early this long," the old timers all said, "well, it can't mean anything but bad."

"You watch," another would snort, "it'll rain all summer 'cause you're havin' your summer now!"

We enjoyed each beautiful day thoroughly, however; it was balm to our spirits after the winter we had experienced that we'd been told would be just like Seattle's! "Yeah! This winter was just like Seattle's winter all right, Tom, when Seattle had its last ice age, that is!" I snorted and guffawed at my own joke. Tom only shook his head in pity.

With the approach of my mother's visit came the offer I'd been hoping for—I was offered a secretarial job at the mill, one of the few prime jobs in town. I accepted eagerly and began a new set of calculations about when we could pay off the boat. At this point, we really did not know what our plans included. Originally we had hoped to pay *Cabaret* off in August and then I supposed we would probably stay a "bit" longer and earn some cruising money. We were not enthusiastic about spending another god-forsaken winter seeing our boat ice up and destroyed before our very eyes. We talked longingly of returning to the San Juans and working where winter weather could be counted on to be bad for only a few weeks instead of months, but now my new job made us think twice about such a plan.

Meanwhile, my mother and step-father were on their way to Wrangell, and Tom and I wondered what their reaction would be to the tiny town we'd chosen to live in. My mother was a city person and for years had a home overlooking the growing metropolis of Portland, and I feared Wrangell would strike her as exceedingly primitive at best. It did. She was not in town two hours when she offered to advance us a loan to pay off the boat so we could leave. It was hard to make her understand Wrangell as we saw it: for us it was an adventure, an experience. Perhaps it was because we knew that we really could leave at any time that we never felt stuck or dismayed. We tried to point out its rustic charm, its friendly atmosphere. She looked at me like I was trying to put one over on her. Further, she could not believe that I actually enjoyed being a secretary—something I had despised only a few years earlier when I'd tried it. I told her it was a matter of relativity—that this job was heaven relative to the other jobs available in town.

Because of my pleasure in the new job we began definitely to plan on staying another full year in Wrangell to obtain cruising funds rather than leave excellent paying jobs in the fall and have to rush south before the bad weather set in. The only hesitation we had in staying was in the boat's ability to stay dry. We lamented at length not having installed a diesel cookstove, but how were we to have foreseen the need for one when we'd been told by literally everybody who'd gone to Alaska that the weather was like Seattle's? Tom discovered the answer one day, however, when he said, "All those people who said the weather here was like Seattle's never spent a winter here, Becky. Think about it. All they ever did was come up here for the summer, and I suppose a two week vacation here in the summer could lead one to believe the weather was the same."

He was right of course. What fools we'd been not to think of this before. But this knowledge did not help us now, for we had a decision to make regarding the boat's heating if we were going to stay. With only a year left we did not want to go to the expense of putting in a diesel cookstove, for we planned on cruising well south of Alaska and knew a diesel stove would be too much for the tropics. We had taken our wall mounted kerosene heater out after replacing the burner three times and the hose twice. The third burner had been defective also and had shot flaming diesel out onto our settee one night, burning cushions and making a terrible mess. The Sharp heater the Smalley's had given us had put out the BTU's well, but we had been forced to burn diesel number one in it instead of kerosene and there is a difference despite what many fuel places will try to tell you! The heater gave off a distinctively strong fuel odor along with a great deal of carbon monoxide when run on plain diesel.

We finally decided on a woodburning stove, and after a lot of research and letter writing, we opted for a Gypsy cast iron wood burning stove. Wood scraps were certainly free and available from the boatyard! We did some remodeling of the interior to accommodate the stove by changing our U-shaped dinette to an L-shaped one and making a tiny tile hearth on the vacated seat next to the bulkhead. We cut the table at an angle and made a wood bin with a side entrance in the storage area beneath the hearth. We put in a heat shield trimmed in iron bark, which never got more than lukewarm, and we awaited the arrival of our stove and pipe on the Foss Alaska Lines from Seattle. The stove made a world of difference the next winter, for *Cabaret* would never again know ice or frost on the interior!

Instead, we would sit about in t-shirts, literally, with ports and hatches open while a blizzard raged away. The remodeling did eliminate the use of the table area as a full bed, and it did make it tight quarters for four people to sit in the dining area.

In June Nancy Smalley came for a week's visit. It was wonderful to see a familiar face again! We took her fishing, to see the petroglyphs, and on a run up the Stikine River to the Garnet Ledge. It's a good thing she was along, for neither Tom nor I knew what garnets looked like. She spotted the first ones for us and quickly I became stricken with garnet fever. As I greedily crawled about scooping up the little gems, all I could say was, "I've got garnet fever!" over and over again.

Toward the end of June the boatyard went to five days a week, nine hours a day, which enabled us to spend our weekends gunkholing around the area. A weekend may not sound like much time, but in Alaska the summer days are so long that it is more like having a three day weekend. We would leave our moorage Friday nights by five and head for our destination. We had until about 11:00 to get settled, for it was still light enough to get situated in an anchorage then. Within six hours of Wrangell there are hundreds of areas one can explore! I would get good suggestions from my fellow employees at the mill, and they never led me wrong, except their fishing hints were lousy. Every Monday I'd return to the office to hear them talk of all the fish they'd snared that weekend. Sometimes they'd ask me how we'd done—believe me, I didn't want to volunteer about our failure. After a while they quit asking and figured I'd tell them if we ever caught any. By the end of the summer I had a whopper of my own to tell...finally. Pretty poor showing though for a couple who lived almost exclusively on a fish diet for several years! Anyway, we vowed we'd go to a different spot each weekend, but some spots were so great that we found we went back to them several times.

One of our favorite areas was along the back channel behind Wrangell Island. We spent several weekends at Madan Bay where we finally found where the biggest Dungeness in the world lived. We didn't discover the area, though, until one of our last trips to Madan Bay right before we left Wrangell. Farther along the same route was Berg Bay, another favorite spot of ours. It had an abandoned gold mine near it, and we spent considerable time clamoring through the woods looking for the Berg mine. We panned gold in a stream there, but Tom never felt at ease panning when I was on guard duty with the rifle on the lookout for bear. He would complain about where I was pointing the gun, how I carelessly swung it about, and my general inattention to predators since I was always monitoring his pan for large gold nuggets.

On the other side of Berg Bay was Aaron's Creek, and we liked to run our Avon along the sloughs to see how far we could get. Further along the channel was the Anan area, an area loaded with anchorages, so no matter which direction the wind, one could just about always find a secure anchorage. The biggest problem was the water depth and the amount of old logging equipment and snags on the bottom. Depending on your keel, it is not advisable to anchor in Alaska in water less than thirty to forty feet, unless you are positive what stage the tide is, for tides can fluctuate perhaps twenty-four feet. It is difficult to find shallow anchorages, anyway. About the shallowest we were able to anchor in was eight fathoms. Often we anchored in twelve to fifteen fathoms, so it was necessary to have lots of anchor chain and line onboard. I once had a salesman in Portland look at me like I was out of my mind (which is true sometimes) because we carried a 35 pound CQR, 100 feet if chain, and 300 feet of line on our main anchor on a 34 foot light displacement boat. I only smiled at his mockery, for I knew in our travels we have anchored in 40 to 45 knot winds behind Port Orford on the Oregon coast and anchored in williwaws up to 50 knots in fjords in Alaska, and not dragged anchor; I doubt he could say the same. He'd have really smirked had he known we also carried a 45 pound Danforth with 30 feet of chain and 250 feet of line, and a baby 13 pound Danforth with 10 feet of chain and 200 feet of line...our lunch hook.

In the other direction from Wrangell we enjoyed St. John's on Zarembo Island, and sometimes took a short run only as far as Roosevelt Harbor, a good stop for huckleberry picking. I made pints of huckleberry jam that summer, my first jam making experience ever, and was bragging about my accomplishment at work when one of my fellow workers said, "You don't have to worry about getting enough meat protein this winter anyway."

"What do you mean?"

"Those huckleberries are full of worms. Didn't you see them floating at the surface when you soaked them overnight?"

Soak them overnight? I could only see all the pans full of fresh huckleberry cobbler I'd made loaded with worms. I involuntarily looked down at my stomach. "Soak them overnight?"

"Yeah. Just soak them in water overnight and most of the worms will float to the surface."

Fortunately I never found worms in my jam so I figured I'd dissolved them while boiling the berries. But it was true…the next time I soaked the berries overnight, and in the morning, the tub was covered with little, white, wiggly worms.

Sometimes we had three-day weekends which, of course, seemed like four days , and once we took a four day weekend and make a trek out to Pt. Baker and Port Protection. Gale warnings were forecast the day we left, but we left anyway hoping it would blow over before we returned. Bad thinking…every time. We sailed the 40 miles out to Pt. Baker in six hours. It would take us over twelve hours to sail back.

The notorious Pt. Baker at last! It is a popular gathering place for fishermen in the summer, and tales of various peoples' exploits there keep people around Wrangell amused all winter. I have to admit, I was disappointed when I saw it, for I had expected something a little different after all the great stories I'd heard and after reading Joe Upton's description of it in his beautiful book, *Alaska Blues*. I was sorry to see the place so filthy with garbage for one thing. The dock was literally covered with refuse of every kind. The bar, somehow standing on the dock, had an unusual character to it though, and I only wished someone like Jack London could spend a winter tucked away in the room slugging away whiskey and fermenting a tale of Alaskan bravado. We gaped at the occupants of the bar, bought a couple of pints of ice cream from the store side of the saloon, and left to exchange ideas on whether what we'd seen could possibly be THE Pt. Baker we'd heard so much about.

The next day we went around the corner to Port Protection and Wooden Wheel Cove and thought it to be a place we'd both like to spend a winter sometime. It was all those things you think of when you try to picture a tiny Alaskan hamlet—other than Meyers Chuck, of course.

In August my father and stepmother came for a visit and, having both secured a few days off work, we awaited their arrival with great anticipation. We had experienced rain for all of May and June, and a fair share of July, so now we prayed the weather would be at least half decent for their four day visit. They brought the sunshine with them, I guess, for we actually had twenty-six days without rain, beginning with their arrival. We bundled them onto *Cabaret* and took them to Berg Bay where we told them we'd rented an Alaskan condominium for them. Actually it was a Forest Service cabin and they were captivated by the idea of these cabins being all over S.E. for rent for $5.00 a night (needless to say the price is now higher!). After endless conversation and a late dinner of what we told them were Alaskan "trout" (a salmon given to us by a neighboring fisherman) we sent them ashore in the skiff armed with a lantern and a rifle. (We'd taken their suitcase, sleeping bags, and air mattresses ashore earlier.) Exhausted from their trip they slept soundly that night. In the morning Tom and I awoke to see them hunkered over my dad's metal detector looking for gold nuggets. "I don't want to mess with any of that gold dust," my dad kept saying. "I want them real big nuggets!"

We took off for the day in our skiff and buzzed down to Anan with a 20 horse Mercury borrowed from a friend. The humpies were running the stream at Anan, and we'd been told it was an incredible sight. We were all amazed by what we saw. We thought the bay was thick with salmon when we could look into the water and see them swirling and milling everywhere, but when we got to the lagoon and creek we were simply agog. The salmon literally made a carpet across the large stream. The water was black with millions of fish. The fish ladder was packed, all of them seeming to be waiting patiently for their turn to advance to the next level. None of us had ever imagined anything like it. There was nothing but swarms of thousands upon thousands of salmon, all returning to do nature's bidding. The spawning grounds were also filled to capacity, and I didn't see how those at the end of the line would stand a chance to fulfill their hard earned destiny.

We hiked to the bear observatory, for bear are thick in the area when the salmon are running, but none of us felt too secure standing about in a large room with no doors or windows. "What's gonna keep those bears from comin' in here and observin'?" someone asked. Nobody had a good answer so we soon left and headed back to the skiff.

We planned on buzzing around to the entrance of the lagoon and letting my dad off on a sandy beach to again seek his fortune with his metal detector. Just as we approached the beach, out of the brush came a nice, big, brown bear loping across the sand chasing seagulls. Tom edged the skiff closer while I grabbed for the camera. We kept up a slow steady approach for a few seconds until my dad yelled out,

"Well, that's close enough, Tom! I can see 'im just fine from right here! You don't need to get any closer!" We all burst into laughter, for this same person, only the day before, had been telling us how he'd like to see a bear and wrestle him right down. Later, of course, his version of the incident became a little distorted as he recounted how he'd tried to jump out of the skiff with a bowie knife between his teeth and wrestle the bear, but how we'd all held him back and refused to get any closer. No wonder I'm such a fabulous liar. It must run in the family!

We returned to *Cabaret* in the evening, and once again my Dad and stepmother went ashore at dark to stay in their cabin. Only it seems they didn't sleep so soundly this time…seems they kept hearing bear noises outside.

Back in Wrangell the next day we took them on a short tour, set them up in the local motel, and began dreading the next day, for it would be their last to spend with us. But the day came sure enough, and we took them to the garnet ledge since we had a good tide for the trip and their flight did not leave until late in the afternoon. They too found the ledge fascinating and my dad found huge pockets of garnets in the streambed with his metal detector set on mineral. For somebody who hated cold water he'd had his shoes off almost continually, wading around in various streams looking for gold. Oddly, the cold water didn't seem to bother him a bit!

We saw them off later, with tears, for I felt hideously depressed. The four days had gone so quickly, it hadn't seemed fair. And now they were gone and we were stuck in this end-of-the-world-out-in-the-boondocks-hole. Yes, stuck. We had just found out that *Cabaret* would not be ours in August. It seems there's a rule called the Rule of 78's, which in essence says you pay more interest in the beginning of your loan than you do at the end…sooooo…it would not be until November that we would own our boat. We were caught! We knew we'd be fools to leave now what with having such good jobs, but oh, how we longed to go—if only to Sitka. Anywhere. Of course, we could have left, but we were so close to owning the boat. We knew if we left, it could set us back months. I was bitterly disappointed. And so passed our first year.

A WINTER OF
PROJECTS AND
PLANNING

My SADNESS WAS SHORT LIVED, for when all was said and done I really did not want to return to Oregon yet. I loved Alaska; I liked Wrangell. If anything, I think the disappointment in not getting the boat paid off was responsible for my bad humor. After all, I reasoned, I had a great job, and life was wonderful for Tom and me. We had a lot of friends, and we were having an experience (I kept reminding myself) that millions of people would like to have. In truth, I was becoming very attached to the slow paced, casual way of life in Wrangell. I really did not miss the rat race of civilization. I can see now that we both really needed a trip to the "outside" to set us straight. We needed a temporary respite from the isolation of Wrangell, and a good dose of smog, traffic, and mass murders would have either sent us scuttling back, or the amenities of theaters, restaurants, and various recreational opportunities would have lured us away forever. But we stayed put, and each day I really tried to absorb as much as I could of the things about me so that I could savor every aspect of our life. Who knew if we'd return to this land once we left to go cruising? Sometimes I could not imagine living anywhere else; other times I felt I was giving up too much for what I was getting in return. Always I was probing this inner turmoil: did I love life here—or hate it? Now that twenty odd years have passed I still crave the beauty and peace of the archipelago of S.E. Alaska, and I often wonder how our lives would have differed had we returned to this network of islands and waterways.

September passed without event except that Tom got yet another big raise. We counted the weeks until pay off day. Every week I deposited Tom's paycheck and I watched our account grow. It was an obsession with me, and my conversation was always prefaced with, "As soon as we pay off the boat, we..." I refused to buy grocery items that would have added a rounded appearance to our icebox. I was insane with intensity.

Finally we reached a point where we had only six weeks left. Six little weeks that seemed to stretch on forever. I hated this constant tendency I was developing for living in the future when the boat was paid for. I wanted to live in the NOW.

"Tom," I said one evening. "Why don't we have a series of fiestas or celebrations each week for the next six weeks? That way we can look forward to each week and not look forward to a date six weeks from now. You know, time might pass faster."

"What kind of celebrations are you thinking of?" he asked with a hint of interest.

"Oh, you know, just something unique each week."

"Well, give me an example!"

"Okay," I began, "for example, we could order those new rain-coats we've been wanting and call that week 'Raincoat Regatta'."

"Yeah, go on."

"Well, let's see. Let's make a list of ideas. How about an ice cream fiesta?"

"Sounds good, but what would that be?"

"We can invite everyone who's an ice cream fanatic to bring a gallon of ice cream and we'll provide the topping and champagne and we'll pig out on ice cream!"

"Sounds great!" He was getting enthused now.

"Then we can have 'Little Italy Week'—and we can eat all of our favorite Italian dishes during that week."

"Do you know that many?"

I knew pizza, spaghetti, and lasagna, but I figured we could throw in a couple of Mexican dishes to give it a full week. "Then week four we can have an 'Import Party', and everybody brings their favorite kind of imported beer and some kind of cheese and crackers. Then how about 'Long-Distance-Dial-a-Thon'?"

"I'm scared to ask what that one is," Tom said.

"Naturally we call everybody we know long distance! The last week we'll call 'Saturday Night Fever' and we'll go out to dinner and celebrate the payoff!"

Tom took to my ideas, and so the next six weeks passed quickly. I ordered our rainwear from Seattle and charged it to VISA. We had a sensational pig out on ice cream and champagne. I felt sick for several days.

'Little Italy Week' followed by the 'Import Party' added a few pounds to my frame, for I go into such celebrations with total participation! 'Long Distance Dial-a-Thon' gave us an excuse to call the Olsons and the Hulls along with everybody else in my phone directory. They seemed shocked to hear from us by phone—as though they were surprised we actually had phones up there in Alaska. Finally came 'Saturday Night Fever', but neither of us felt like nursing a hangover the next day, so we didn't get too feverish in ordering our drinks!

It finally happened: one year and three months after our arrival in Wrangell, I sent in a check for $24,000 to pay off our boat. We had saved $14,000 in this fifteen month time, and most of that had been from March on. Were we relieved? No. We were tired. We were tired of hoarding every dime and doing without things that I felt we were entitled. As a reaction (albeit a foolish one) to our self-imposed deprivation, I went on a spending spree that would literally take us months to recover from. I ordered items from marine catalogues like crazy, charging all to VISA, of course. And I really surprised Tom when he came home one night and I showed him airline tickets to Portland for Christmas, again compliments of VISA.

Our icebox was now loaded with imported beers, delicatessen treats, and exotic fresh produce (well, as fresh as it could get at the time). I thought absolutely nothing of prices and did my shopping as though I were Mrs. Got Bucks. Huge parcels from marine stores began arriving, and with glee we'd go through items in the boxes: taffrail log, new masthead light with strobe, rocker stoppers, shackles, line, all nice new toys.

I ordered shorts and sandals in preparation for our cruise. We sent all our cushions away to be re-covered and new foam put in. We made new boat curtains, and I bought all new dishes, giving my stoneware ones away. In short, we went from one extreme to the other. It felt great. Vaguely, I knew we would have to put a halt to this if we were ever going to save any money to cruise on, but I kept rationalizing my expenditures by saying we might as well buy all these things while we had jobs.

When we went south for Christmas I again rationalized my extravagance by saying that since it was costing us so much to get there anyway we might as well go whole hog. We did. We made list upon list of things to be sure and buy while "out" and other lists were composed for things to take south—some to leave there permanently; one of which things was Annie. We had wrestled with this decision at great length. We really enjoyed Annie, but it was obvious that this was no life for her. Never in the time we'd been in Wrangell had she gone ashore. Too many dogs and dock cats kept her a virtual prisoner on *Cabaret*. Her litter box was kept outside, and that comprised the extent of her wanderings. To use it, however, she usually had to battle other dock cats who, along with their owners, apparently thought it was a public cat restroom. We were sick and tired of other cats on our boating fighting with her. (Tom was not nicknamed "Cat Killer" for no reason!) We knew too that with her inability to get sea legs it would be best to find a home for her before we left to travel. So with great reluctance we borrowed a cat carrier and made reservations for Annie to go south with us—one way only.

Suffice to say that our trip to Portland was a whirlwind of hedonism and culture shock. We had been out of civilization (as the lower 48 knows it) for a year and a half, but it might as well have been a decade. We sat in a lounge at Seattle's SeaTac and stared about us like hicks. There we were in long underwear, flannel shirts, levis, and hiking boots in a room full of people who looked like they'd just stepped out of Vogue. There were more people in the lounge alone than in all of Wrangell. We tried unsuccessfully not to gape.

Our two weeks in Portland flew by. It was tough to leave the unseasonably balmy weather Portland was having, and we returned to Wrangell as though we had a prison term to finish, but with a list of projects to accomplish before we could leave on the cruise. Since January and February were not good outside project months, we ordered our new transmission and installed it. We had hoped to get by with just new clutch plates, but when the mill mechanic went to press the housing apart he broke it and we soon found ourselves having to pack up the whole gear box to send to Seattle. The gearbox housing had seized up due to overheating. We figured that the vibrations from the previously loose stern bearing and four years of freewheeling under sail had probably caused the problem. Repairing the problem 1,000 miles away from knowledgeable help was another matter. By the time it was all repaired we both felt we were experts on Paragon gears.

We attended Wrangell's First Annual Tent City Festival in January, celebrating the time when Wrangell had been a tent city of over 15,000 gold prospectors. It was a fabulous weekend of beard judging, long underwear outfits, and tall tales. My favorite event was the tall tale one (of course, since I am a natural born tale teller like my dad). The tall tales were told by some of the most practiced tale tellers in all of Southeast Alaska. In the smoky backroom of the Totem Bar an awed audience listened to Robin Taylor, Wrangell's judge, and Jack Shay, Ketchikan's mayor, whip out some of the most far fetched, dramatic, arresting stories ever heard. It was a weekend of character and fun, supported by large numbers of visitors from Ketchikan and Petersburg. Alaskans love nothing better than a festive occasion to brighten the long, dark, cold winters.

We went to the 'Fireman's Ball', a gala event in which formals and levis are equally received when Wrangell's excellent volunteer fire and rescue department tend bar and serve drinks for one night while the town turns out en masse to support them. This affair is followed by the 'Fishermen's Brawl' held at a local bar.

In March Tom began building our windvane. We had gotten the plans from a friend who vowed that it worked like a charm. We also pulled the mast and mounted our new masthead light. We bought an R.D.F. and I began reviewing celestial navigation (yup—the days before GPS!). We ordered charts and more charts, and we sold our aluminum skiff and bought an 8' aquadory that fit easily on the foredeck. I sent our mainsail to Seattle to get another set of reef points put in, and we rebedded stancheons and recaulked deck boxes and hatches. In short, we were preparing for our cruise. It was a time of great excitement and yet some nostalgia too. We would be saying goodbye to people we'd grown to like, and we stood a chance of never seeing them again. I wanted to remember these people and this town, for they had taken us in and had been good to us. Tom had profited immensely from his work at the boatyard, and he would miss the group of guys he'd drunk coffee and rolled oakum with.

It was time to leave, and though we were leaving with a significant amount of money less than what we'd hoped, due to my spending sprees, we had to make the break. We both knew if we didn't go now, we might never leave.

Tom's parents, Iva and Jerry, came for a visit the last week we were in Wrangell and planned on accompanying us to Sitka, one of many stops we had not made that we had always wanted to make. I had firmly urged them not to bring any extra luggage, so I was quite chagrined when we met them at the ferry terminal and they each had two large suitcases and a crate of fresh oranges. I could just see us under sail with baggage tied on deck flapping away in the breeze. Nevertheless we tried to make the best of a tight situation. We had never had guests aboard before for more than a day or two, so this was a test of our good humor and hospitality having four adults living in a 34' boat for a week. After this experience we adopted the motto: cocktails for six, dinner for four, sleeps two! I know they felt somewhat out of their element, but we all made the best of the week they were with us, and we were able to show them some of our favorite places, including Petersburg, Thomas Bay (replete with ghost stories) and Warm Springs Bay, one of my personal favorites.

It had been a long run from Thomas Bay to Warm Springs Bay, so when we finally tied to the dock we were ready for the nice hot mineral baths. The bath house was an old, long building with a series of small bathing rooms. Some of the tubs were huge cattle water troughs; others were like big long wooden boxes. Hot smelly water ran in them continually, and after a short time we were beet red, and I felt parboiled. The bay is a favorite stop for many fishermen, we found out, who stop on their way north to fish and then stop again on the return trip south. I was wondering if they bathed anywhere in between, but I didn't ask.

Warm Springs Bay was a beautiful area and the weather was spectacular. Tom went for a swim in the icy waters of the lake, and Jerry caught some marvelous Dolly Varden at the base of the falls. We were so impressed by the regal, snow-covered mountains that predominate on Baranof Island, and both Tom and I felt it was about the most beautiful and aptly named island that we'd seen in Southeast.

After two days we turned *Cabaret* up Chatham for Peril Strait. We wanted to make a stop or two before we reached Sitka on the 12th when Iva and Jerry had a plane to catch. The remaining trip to Sitka was beautiful but uneventful other than being passed by a large school of killer whales while waiting for slack water to navigate the narrows. Sitka was wonderful, but Tom was still adamant about not wanting to live in Alaska again. I felt Sitka had future promise, however. We were both fascinated by an idea we'd hatched about taking a year and going into the wilds to live on our boat. The outside coast of Baranof Island seemed the best area to do it in, for the milder climate along the coast would generally keep the bays ice free. We studied the charts of the area carefully and found hundreds of anchorages with good protection, fresh water streams, and what looked like good fishing and hunting. We were tempted to give our pioneering efforts at living in the wild a trial that year, but I guess we were both looking forward to warm weather for awhile. We were enthralled by the idea of a year in the wilds, though, and I believe we will do it yet before we end our boating career.

Tom's parents took our good weather with them when they left Sitka, for it began to blow southerly and now we had to play The Waiting Game, a game neither my husband nor I do well. We did not want to head down the outside coast in a southerly gale, however, so we saw Sitka in minute detail and tried, as I think of it, to rest up in advance. After four days we could stand it no more. The storm was abating so we left despite the southerly winds and swell. Our first day was actually not bad. We made about 40 miles beating before the winds got so light that we could not make any headway against the seas. We sought out a nearby anchorage and ended up finding it so captivating that we spent an extra day. The bottom fishing was terrific and the sea life was fascinating. We rowed about for hours staring at the colorful world below us that we'd not seen for two years. The outside coast had a tremendous amount of more visible sea life than the inner islands seemed to, largely due to the amount of milky glacial water around Wrangell, I think.

We left to a flat sea and sunny skies. The water was almost oily it was so calm. We motored along in t-shirts marveling continually at the incredible beauty of Baranof Island. Despite the plenitude of anchorages, the day was so spectacular that we kept on traveling, enjoying the scenery and the dolphin that raced along beneath the bow of our boat. I am convinced that dolphin know if you are watching them or not, for I have found that when one of us goes forward and watches them they stay with the boat much longer and demonstrate brilliant maneuvers. When we ignore them they seem to quit performing much sooner.

We rounded Cape Ommaney in awe as we saw the navigational lights perched high atop the gigantic rock and saw remains of lights that had been battered out by 90 foot seas. Here we were motoring by in such a calm that we could have rowed the skiff over to climb the cape had we the inclination. I could see where Cape Ommaney could indeed be ominous in a storm all right.

Our next stop, Port Alexander, was a little hamlet about five miles from the tip of Baranof. We'd heard it was a pretty area with a colorful past. We were surprised by the number of new houses and the youth of most of the inhabitants.

"Yep, population of 106 with three in the basket," the 'mayor' of Port Alexander told us. We'd read that at one time more beer was consumed, per capita, in Port Alexander than anywhere else in the world, but we saw no evidence of this, for there was not a bar or liquor store in sight. "We make our own home brew," the mayor informed us. "It tastes okay once you get used to it." Unfortunately, his supply had vanished, so we didn't get a sample. We resisted his sales pitch about the boatyard that was available when he found out Tom was a shipwright. "We could always use a good school teacher too," he added to me as an additional, but completely unnecessary bit of bait. "We have a nice school building and have a movie once a month! And you are in luck 'cause tonight we are showing Perils of Pauline." We graciously declined his offer since I'd seen it several times decades ago.

The sail across the Bay of Iphegenia was one I'll never forget, for in our excitement and pleasure at having a downwind sail we failed to heed the increasing wind and sea conditions. We were racing along hitting eight and often nine knots, surfing off of swells. Increasingly the boat began to career out of control, but after Tom reefed the main we figured we were set for some more good running. Within ten minutes we were again out of control. Instead of reefing a second time Tom just took the main down and we planned on running under just the jib. As he was securing the main I glanced again at the knot meter to see it climbing steadily from 7.5 to 8, on to 8.5 then 8.8 knots. Just as we hit 9.2 knots there was a loud crashing and banging forward. The smaller wisker pole we'd been using had broken loose from the mast, tearing the sheet out of the cam cleat and ripping a splice out of the ½" line at the foot of the sail. Tom was on deck dodging a wildly flailing aluminum pole. Suddenly I became very aware of how incredibly rough the seas and wind had become, for an 8 foot swell with a 3 to 5 foot chop was making it impossible to turn the boat up into the wind for Tom to grab the sail so we could get it down. We finally had to lower the sail, pole and all, into the water to gain any control of the thrashing weapon. We hanked on our four year old unused storm sail and finished the bay off at 5 knots. Once in the Bay of Esquibel we raised the jib again, but we prudently held back on the main. Our prudence was rewarded, for once again we charged off between 6 and 7 knots, but the winds were dying and the sea in Esquibel amounted to only about a 3 foot wind chop so we sailed at ease. We talked fleetingly of a cabin in the mountains and momentarily regretted our time and effort to pay off the boat.

By the time we were secured to the dock in the small town of Craig, we could talk of the incident a little more calmly and objectively and realized the truth in the statement that the only difference between having too much wind and having a nice sail is the amount of sail up. We had covered 90 miles in 12 hours, however. Quite a day! The following day we trolled down to Waterfall and caught a huge sea bass. We anchored in Bocas Point and heard with dismay a forecast for a southerly gale.

Despite the forecast, we were determined to reach Elbow Bay the next day, but we never made it, for the wind and seas in the Bay of Cordova made progress almost impossible. For the first time ever we turned *Cabaret* around and backtracked. We headed for an anchorage by Cocoa Harbor that looked promising and protected, but the hidden anchorage we discovered was as beautiful as anything we've ever seen. After entering through a 20 foot wide, very shallow entrance, a spectacular "lagoon" completely surrounded by wooded mountains greeted us. Not a breath of wind stirred, while outside the lagoon the wind was blowing 25 knots and the seas were sloppy. We were positively enchanted with the beauty and peace before us, so we stayed on for several days, exploring and luxuriating in the green splendor.

We left our unnamed lagoon with Nicholas Bay at Cape Chacon as our probable destination. It was a beautiful day with light and variable winds, so we sailed along slowly, or not at all sometimes, and enjoyed thoroughly the indescribable land we were seeing. We talked of our impending trip through Canada, and I could not get fresh oysters out of my mind. I had Tom dig out my snorkeling gear to make sure it was in good order, and I became impatient to see Desolation Sound again and swim in the warm waters there. I put my mask and snorkel on for a time and sat in the cockpit wishing the long miles away, dreaming again of finding ancient artifacts in the waters of Prideaux Haven. When I checked the weather that afternoon I heard the dismal news that another southerly was on its way. We could be held up at Nicholas Bay for weeks—why not head across Dixon Entrance that day? "Tom, what do you think about just keeping going?" I asked. "The weather sounds bad for a crossing if we wait." I knew we could make it across Dixon Entrance before the storm hit, and if we didn't go now it could be a week or more laying at anchor waiting.

"Let's go for it," Tom said. So we set sail for a night crossing of Dixon Entrance and our departure from Alaska. Our winds died on us about 10 that night and the swell picked up, so it was a very rocky passage. About midnight I was on watch, and as I turned to cast one parting glance, I saw the last streaks of a brilliant sunset outlining dramatically the dark coast. Ahead the sky was black with night, and so I bid goodnight and farewell to the land I had come to both love and hate.

ON LEAVING FROM CAPE CHACON

Farewell Land of the Midnight Sun
Land of the Endless Rain
Land of the Driving Cold
In you have I known a lonely joy.
Not for everyman a silent land,
Nor for everyman the inside seas,
Only those who stay may conquer these—
Or conquered be.
6/24/80

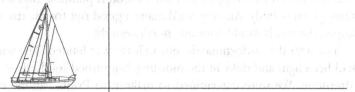

HOMECOMING

W<small>E RAISED HEADSAIL ABOUT</small> 5 A.M. in the tumultuous Hecate Strait and drove *Cabaret* hard all day. It was clear and exceedingly windy with capping seas, and we flew southward, never again looking back. All day we sailed at top speeds. We had planned on going straight through to Port Hardy, but by afternoon we were tired from having to be constantly on the wheel because the windvane blade was too heavy a gauge aluminum to steer the boat without the boat yawing. Tom picked out a little niche out of the now howling northwest winds and set anchor. He commemorated our being in Canada by diving overboard while I rummaged for something to eat besides sandwiches. A cautionary word needs to be inserted here about my husband's ability to dive into frigid waters. Since I have known Tom, which as of this writing is now 30 years, the man has gone swimming in the most unlikely of waters. From the frigid lakes of Alaska, to the calm of the North Pacific high, Tom has ventured overboard. And what's really pathetic, is that he has continuously, for 30 years, conned me into joining him! "It's not cold, Becky. Honestly." He says this every time, and every time I fall for it, much like poor Charley Brown who has the football jerked from under him every fall by Lucy in the Peanuts cartoon strip. Now, of course, I have added to my misery by deciding that I will know when I am an old lady when I think the water is too cold to go swimming. Why did I do that to myself? When I stall, Tom does not hesitate to ask if perhaps I am getting too old. There is nothing like jumping overboard thinking the water isn't "too bad" to find that one's heart has stopped and one's blood is pumping backwards through one's body. Anyway, we'd made a good run for the day and hoped the winds would continue northwesterly.

The next day, unfortunately, our mileage was limited. The winds had been light and fluky in the morning, but turned southerly in the afternoon. We were determined to make it to Pruth Bay the next day, however.

We left in fog early the next morning and had to motor well into Laredo Sound before the wind came up. The day was gray and ugly and the wind was very gusty once it got started. We decided to cut across Millbank Sound and head down the inside rather than chance an impending storm. We were both tired and didn't relish beating into a storm in Hecate Straight if we didn't have to. The winds held well and we were able to sail down the inside channels until off Namu. We finally turned the motor on and at long last straggled into Pruth Bay. We had gone over 120 miles, mostly under sail, in 14 hours, and we were exhausted. We felt we deserved an extra day at one of our favorite stops, so we stayed and rested up at Pruth Bay for our last northern crossing: Queen Charlotte Sound.

Pruth Bay had originally been recommended to us by boaters we'd met two years previous when we'd been northbound. When we first stopped on our way north we could not figure out why they thought it such a spectacular stop. It was a nice anchorage, but hardly one you would oooh and aaah over, or so we thought. Once we went ashore, however, and began to make our way through the woods we began to discover why this anchorage was so spectacular. On the half mile walk from the anchorage to the beautiful sandy cove on the other side of the isthmus, there were indeed marvels to see. A beautiful mask carving complete in three dimension was about 20 or 30 feet up one tree. The mask was carved and painted right into the tree's trunk. Farther on there was a tree whose trunk made a perfect circle in the middle. But the best, for me, was the unbelievable sandy cove that the trail finally led to. The white sandy beach was undisturbed by human footprints and the surf was nil.

The first time we'd stumbled out into the cove we'd been plain flabbergasted and had combed the entire length of the beach poking into recesses and clamoring over rocks leading to other isolated coves. We felt like Robinson Crusoe and had gone native and enjoyed a brief skinny dip. The water had not been too bad (Tom would say it was great) so we'd splashed around until I began to worry about someone coming along. Two years later we stood on the same sandy beach and could not resist the urge to tear off our clothes and to race to the water. We only did a token amount of swimming, for there were several boats anchored where we were and I knew I'd either be embarrassed to death or freeze in the water if they came across us. "If we ever come this way again we've got to stop here and do this again," I said to Tom. It seemed like tradition now.

The Queen Charlotte crossing was unpleasant, as we'd expected. Moderate seas on the beam kept us rolling. I thought I was miserable until I saw two tugs trying to head north. When I saw the bows of the boats rising and then deeply plunging into the seas I knew somebody was suffering more than I was. It was 12 hours we simply had to grit our teeth and endure. We talked again about cabins in the mountains. Off watch it was too rolly for me to read, so I slumped forlornly outside and watched the gray seas and sky and waited for my next stint on the wheel.

We arrived at Port Hardy and I immediately set off to get customs for clearance. Unfortunately, Port Hardy no longer cleared vessels, so we were given a temporary clearance to get us to Campbell River. We weren't very happy about the situation, for we had looked forward to spending time wandering about the northern islands before we went into Desolation Sound. There was nothing we could do about it now, though, so once more we hurriedly headed out in the morning for a 106 mile run to Campbell River. So much for the crab at Pott's Lagoon that I had dreamed about!

We stopped at Kanish Bay that night, for we wanted to have the exact tide to maneuver through Seymour Narrows. We had had a brilliant day of sailing, and Tom had finally realized a two year dream of sailing DOWN Johnstone Straits. Heading north we had had to motor against a howling northwester, and we had watched in envy as sailboats had peacefully glided by going the other direction. Now Tom's turn to glide by the other suffering souls was at hand, but we saw only two souls that day. Nevertheless it had been great and he had gloated cheerfully.

At long last, the dreaded Seymour Narrows would not be forestalled. I nervously licked my lips as I felt the boat being sped along by the current. Seymour had a history of fearful whirlpools sucking huge fishing vessels down, down, down, according to our fishing friends in Newport. The authorities had blasted out the submerged rock, however, that had caused drownings and capsizings, but still the horror stories lived on and I remembered all the terrible details with total recall. "Hang on," I hollered (quite unnecessarily for it was calm and the current had all but ceased at slack water.) "Here we go, Tom! This is the biggy!" And we both started laughing, for there was absolutely nothing! We motored on past an exodus of northbound boats and ferries and laughed at our wasted nervousness. Tom went below to shower, and I was alone on deck to experience the dizzying currents and chop off Race Point. "Yikes!" I shouted to myself, trying to keep *Cabaret* headed the right direction.

"What's going on up there?" Tom yelled from the confines of the shower as the boat was jiggling and dancing about the chop.

"N-n-n-nothing," I answered while we continued to careen from side to side.

We cleared customs at Campbell River and treated ourselves to breakfast out. We spent the day doing laundry, exchanging paperbacks at a used bookstore, and obtaining a Canadian fishing license. Another southerly blew in before we could get away. This one packed quite a good punch with it, so we contented ourselves to stay at the dock. We saw more of Campbell River than we really cared to and waited for the winds to cease howling at gale force strength up the Straits of Georgia. "This sure isn't anything like the weather I remember from two years ago," Tom commented. We couldn't get over the constant procession of southerlies.

"Summer in Alaska was as good as this," I added. "We should have stayed up there!" I was not only disappointed about the weather, but I was almost heartbroken over news of the red tide that had invaded the oyster territory. After two years of dreaming and longing, it didn't seem fair.

The storm passed quickly and we headed impatiently for Refuge Cove, for we were anxious to see the Smalleys and the Hulls. Finally, Tom spotted Nancy first, who was waving and running about the dock like a wild woman looking for a place for us to tie. I saw the Hulls on *Osprey* and we could hardly wait to get in. It was so good to see these people again! Our chance reunion had worked out. We'd had boaters and fishermen all along our trip south relaying messages, sometimes to total strangers to relay, that we would try to be in Refuge Cove on

July 4th. We'd made it. I was so happy to see everyone that I found it difficult to finish any one sentence without bursting into a new one!

The next day we left with *Turtle* and *Osprey* for Prideaux Haven. Though it was overcast and chilly, I still jumped overboard in memory of old times. We could not get used to the number of boaters anchored there, however, for our two years in Alaska had spoiled us with privacy. We fished and caught a goodly number of rock cod, but we felt somewhat disappointed in our return. Our memories had tricked us, and what with the lack of good weather, lack of edible oysters, and overabundance of fellow boaters, our return trip was very anticlimactic. We followed Craig's suggestion next, and we went up to the very end of Pendrell Sound, a place he and Molly had delighted in when they'd last visited the area. It was splendid, for the only boats there were ours and the weather cleared off to be sunny and hot. Tom and I spent two days snorkeling and laying our pasty white bodies in the sun. The heat of the sun felt delicious, and I knew I was overdoing it for my first exposure in two years; we both burned, a rare thing for me, and I peeled for weeks, but it had felt so good I rationalized it was worth it.

Squirrel Cove was our next stop while enroute to Fred and Nancy's selection of the Octopus Islands. Octopus Islands are a park situated in the central area of all the worst rapids, but Tom and I felt at ease about rapid running since the big Seymour Narrows had been such a snap. Getting through Hole-in-the Wall was not fun, however. Even at what was to be slack water the current was boiling and swirling through the opening. Sometimes *Cabaret* got caught in the current's grip and the boat would sideslip before our 6.5 knot speed could gain us steerage.

Octopus Islands were beautiful, but rainy dull weather kept us from swimming. We went out exploring in our skiff one day and had a good time despite the rain. Mostly we visited with our friends, though, for when we left Octopus Islands we would be saying goodbye again—who knew for how long. We had to get south. We wanted to spend several weeks in Oregon seeing family and friends and readying *Cabaret* for her trip, and we knew from past experience that it would be wise to get off the Oregon coast by the end of August. (As it turned out, we left off the coast August 23rd, only two days before the first southerlies began blowing that year.)

We all left the next morning with *Cabaret* leading the way through Surge Narrows and Beazley Pass (should be called Beastly).

We honked farewell to Fred and Nancy and sailed along with *Osprey* to Cape Mudge. There they made a turn for Campbell River and we headed down the Straits of Georgia.

The weather was poor so we moved right along making full day runs. We stopped briefly at Kuleet Bay, the scene of our anchor and chain fatality two years before. We tried to recollect where we'd been, but things had changed along the shoreline. We dropped only our lunch hook while Tom dove to see if by some miracle the anchor might be found. We left, breathing a sigh of genuine relief to have escaped without losing anything else. The place seemed cursed to us, so we went on to Montague Harbor, looking forward to hiking again across the scenic island and picnicking at one of the campsites.

Finally we crossed into the American San Juans and headed for Friday Harbor and customs. Our week in Friday Harbor was sunny and warm and we were able to accomplish a lot. We spent a week in the quaint town putting the finishing touches on the boat and getting it hauled for a bottom paint job. We replaced the 1/8" aluminum blade on our windvane with .040 and hoped it would work better. Much to our relief we found the vane performed brilliantly going to windward and on a beam reach. It did very well on a broad reach, but just fair on a run, and that was only until the seas got too big. From what we could ascertain from other boaters it worked at least as well as most other vanes, however.

We left Friday Harbor for Port Angeles and ended up battling against a gale for the last four hours of the trip. It was miserable and we finally could make no headway under sail…even with the engine running full throttle our passage was perilous and painfully slow. We talked once more about the mountain cabin. It took us three hours to cover the last six miles; I will never, ever, forget what that stretch of coastline looks like!

For two days we waited out a gale in Port Angeles. Finally a morning dawned still and dense with fog, but with gale winds predicted for the afternoon. We knew the time of our escape was at hand. We slipped away from the docks and within seconds had lost sight of them. Tom had carefully plotted our courses and e.t.a.'s at each course change, so we proceeded full speed ahead with a cautious eye on the clock and the compass. We ran all day in extremely dense fog, taking RDF fixes at regular intervals to double check our dead reckoning position. We were in the separation zone, we hoped, but we kept a sharp lookout for any looming dark hulls bearing down on us. Miraculously the fog lifted and the wind sprang up when we were about 100 yards off Sail Rock. We cheerfully finished off the trip into Neah Bay, thankful that the fog had lifted when it did, and glad we'd left when we did, for the wind was soon screaming down the Straits of Juan de Fuca again.

The next morning we slipped out behind Tatoosh Island and set sail for Newport. The weather magically cleared and we had a great day of downwind sailing. Soon we were reducing sail, for the northwesters were howling. We ticked off our landmarks and pitied the boats we saw beating themselves senseless trying to head north. The day slowly wore away, and night found us sailing at 7 knots under a reefed main. The winds did not die down, however, and at midnight we double reefed the main and still flew southward at 7 and 7.5 knots. By morning we were off the Columbia River and were able to raise full sail for a few hours, but once the winds built up their momentum again we hauled sails down and continued under a double reefed main. We passed through the Russian fishing fleet off Tillamook Head and we did our bit for détente by waving hello while secretly fearing they might try to run us over. The steady wind was tiring, for we had not been able to set the vane and had had to steer the whole way, taking two hour watches, so we opted to duck behind Cape Lookout to spend the night, then continue on to Newport in the early morning. Getting behind Cape Lookout was not an easy task, however, for the onshore gusts were exceeding 40 knots at the point and the seas were hitting us broadside and slopping into the boat. We were both doused thoroughly.

After a good night's sleep behind the protection of the magnanimous cape, we left at 5 A.M., able to raise full sail. Off Lincoln City we shouted greetings to our former teaching associates and we waited excitedly for Newport finally to become visible past Cape Foulweather. Soon we were reduced to a double-reefed main again, so that when we made our approach to Newport's harbor it seemed more than ever like a haven and refuge. As we passed under the bridge I flung an earring overboard, for its mate had been accidentally dropped in the bay two years ago when we'd left, and I had kept the remaining one, promising that I would fling it into the bay should we ever return. The earring had managed to survive several boat cleaning frenzies, so now it could seek out its companion. Ironically the earrings were in the form of gold doubloons with clipper ships engraved on them.

We arranged for moorage for a month at South Beach Marina. We showered and then set forth in search of old friends. It was good to see Jody, my former roommate/mother/mentor again. She gave us the use of her car and fed us a couple of delicious meals. We spent a night at Paul and Janel's farm, and I laid awake for a long time listening to a mama cow piteously bawling for her calf, wondering if the life we'd chosen was all it was cracked up to be.

We went to Portland that weekend and began the task of provisioning *Cabaret* for a cruise. I always keep a large amount of provisions aboard so that we could survive for some time should the need arise, but it is remarkable how many more items we included. We replenished our dried goods and picked up a goodly supply of canned meats, powdered juices and an assortment of various cleaning products. I finally admitted defeat and we bought an autopilot. It cut a big chunk out of our cruising funds, but it had more than paid for itself by the time we got to San Diego. It made overnight runs a snap and was basically like an extra person as crew...one that didn't eat! It was a good move, and I regretted that we hadn't bought one ages ago when people had recommended it. We bought a chronometer and stopwatch; we had to make a water catcher and get a new windshield made for the dodger. We could not seem to buy enough charts, fishing tackle, and last minute odds and ends. I was learning a great deal about the hidden costs of cruising!

Finally we returned to Newport. The days had passed too quickly. We had not gotten everything done or prepared, but the time for our departure could not be delayed. We selected August 23rd, Tom's birthday, as our tentative departure date, and we tried to prepare accordingly. We had a steady stream of visitors we were delighted to see, for when all was said and done, we finally realized we'd never really get everything ready and prepared all at once for departure anyway. There's always something that is overlooked, so we spent more time visiting and put off some projects for other stops.

The 23rd finally came, and I prepared the quarterberth and called everyone to tell them it looked like all signals were go. We planned to leave Newport in the evening so that if we wanted to stop in Coos Bay we would be there in daylight hours, or if we opted to continue on we would be off Cape Blanco and clear the reefs there during daylight. Chuck and Bea Sholes came over a few hours before we left. We had finally managed to contact them on the radio that day while they were out fishing. They spent our last afternoon in port with us. I was glad we had finally gotten together with them. They helped us pass an otherwise fidgety afternoon and gave us a huge can of peanuts and a bottle of fine wine as a send off.

5:00 came and we fired *Cabaret's* engine up. The wind had come up again rather strongly and the fog was rapidly moving in. A strange combination, and my superstitious mind hoped it would not be a foreboding of a bad trip down the Oregon coast. We cast off, waving goodbye to the rapidly diminishing figures of Chuck and Bea. Our odyssey would continue now and would take us to as yet unknown destinations. As we headed out the jetties I cast a furtive glance back to see Newport being enveloped in a thick fog. "I wonder if we'll ever see it again, Tom." With my mind a jumble of confused thoughts and feelings, we set sail south with a growing aura of excitement, fear, and adventure!

CALIFORNIA
CRUISIN'

OUR PASSAGE THAT NIGHT was fitful and lumpy. The seas, confused and capping, jostled us madly in the dying wind. Even still our new Tillermaster autopilot "Tilly" worked like a champ and we both enjoyed our first night aboard as "passengers". The ugly gray about us, however, what with the mad dancing of the boat and Chuck and Bea's send-off toddy all worked toward making me ill. I suspect a strong case of overly taut nerves contributed too. Morning found us south of Coos Bay by some 18 miles thanks to the current and set we had from the following seas. Our fate was sealed. Bandon, a small bar south of Coos Bay was impassable at the time, so today was the day I'd secretly dreaded for months. Today would be our passage past the frightful Cape Blanco. We had no choice: Coos Bay lay well behind us, and Bandon was closed.

I had feared Cape Blanco for years—still do. It is one of the western most points of the continental United States and has reefs that extend seaward about five miles. Its reputation is ferocious for mighty howling winds and seas of wild frenzy. Well, we might as well get it over with, I thought to myself. Once and for all, one way or the other.

We'd been advised by a large fishing boat headed north that Blanco had been rough that morning when he'd come around it, but

85

he "thought" we could make it. What choice did we have? It was beginning to rage northwesterly again.

I grimly settled in and we forged on. Soon Tom was able to make out the light. "That's it!" I looked ahead to see a long flat point of land with a large lighthouse at its tip. Sky and sea were still gray, although the seas were not yet uncomfortable. I watched in terrified fascination as we crept closer and closer. I couldn't believe my eyes! There were actually fishing boats fishing off the cape.

"They've got to be NUTS!" I said in disbelief.

"Blanco fishermen are about the toughest there are," Tom concurred. "If a guy fishes this area you know he's serious. It's a small hardy handful who do, but they sure have a reputation!"

We passed among them and I watched the now growing seas heaving them high into the air. The wind was picking up, and while my nerves seemed to grow on edge again, the fishermen appeared relatively unperturbed, with only a few beginning to pull in their gear and head for the protective cape of Port Orford—our goal also.

Cutting diagonally across the howling NW gale and building seas towards Port Orford was no easy trick, and we found ourselves taking seas on the beam that sent buckets of water into the cockpit, drenching us and the piles of blankets, pillows, and junk that I had carelessly left strewn all over the cockpit. The going was tough. In my misery I took to the low rail and was sick again. The sick business had to stop, I knew, or I'd never live to get anywhere. Fear and apprehension were my real enemies, not the usual *mal de mer*.

Port Orford, a small city of anchored boats, provided magnificent protection from the seas, but the winds swept the anchorage viciously, gusting to speeds of 40 knots. We, and most of the fleet, spent two days there waiting for the nor'westers to subside a bit before we headed on to Brookings. Meanwhile, we tuned in to channel 68 every day on the VHF and overheard all the local gossip, fish stories, lamentations about the ones that got away and general kibitzing.

Leaving Port Orford at 6:00 A.M. found us under jib alone flying towards Brookings. It promised to be a fine day, though, and we could now look forward to a good night's sleep every night, for we planned to harbor hop the length of the glorious California coast, seeing the sights and watching the Golden State slide by. Now, it takes some doing for a died-in-the-wool Oregonian to concede that California has some enviable features, but by the time we left

California I would have been willing to live there in a heartbeat if I could have afforded it!

Brookings, Crescent City, and Eureka were our next three stops. Nothing spectacular happened in Brookings except they began sending us a bill for $2.50 after we left. They continued this bill for several years—I was never sure what it was for—and when I paid them just to stop getting the mail, they sent me a credit for $2.50. Go figure. In Crescent City we talked with a young man recently arrived by boat from Los Angeles. He advised us not to enter Eureka bar on any tide but a flood or slack. I'd heard stories about the Eureka bar from an old Alaskan acquaintance, a west coast sailor who had single-handedly plied the waters from Mexico to Alaska numerous times. Still I had my doubts. After all, wasn't the Columbia River Bar about the worst in the world? And we'd traversed it many times.

"How many river bars have you ever crossed?" I questioned.

"Eureka was my first and I hope my last!" he responded.

Ah! That explained it! No experience! "Well," I pompously began, "in Oregon all we have are river bars, so we're used to them. In fact, the worst bar in the whole world, the Columbia River Bar, is right in Oregon! I mean it's sooooo bad that huge ships have to lay outside in stormy weather and wait to get in! I'm sure Eureka isn't worse than that!"

Out of courtesy we agreed that it was advisable not to enter except on a flood or slack, but then I realized that would put us entering in the dark! Sometimes I wonder if entering in the dark might not have been better! The bar was bad on an ebb, and it was augmented by the eel grass that poured out with the river that wound tightly around our prop causing us to cavitate badly and not make any headway. As we drifted towards the jetty, Tom finally had to back down hard in reverse to free the prop so we could make some forward progress. I promise I'll listen next time, I told myself.

We were greeted in Eureka by a barrage of cruisers and would-be cruisers who immediately set about learning our planned destiny, life histories and personal anecdotes. We had been contemplating jumping off for Hawaii from Eureka until we were bombarded with a litany of "You've got to be kidding!" and "You're nuts if you go now!" and similar exclamations. Too late in the year! Too rough! Too too too. Of course none of them had ever made the trip, but they'd all *read* about it. Hadn't we *read* anything they asked us incredulously? My ego wanted to play the game of one upsmanship and ask just where they had cruised (not at all) but I bit my tongue. We *had* been hesitant to leap off for Hawaii from so far north so late in the year. "Well, maybe we should listen for once, Tom. It won't hurt us to go further south before we leave, and we'd contemplated going south anyway." After talking with the owner of *Barnaby*, a Cal-46 who did have a history of sailing experience, we decided to go south—way south. He recommended San Diego, or better yet, Cabo San Lucas—next May.

The morning we left we were again admonished—this time for leaving in the fog. But we left, fog and all. Slack water though. Had we waited for the fog to lift we might well have wintered in Eureka, for the wind turned off and the fog turned on from Eureka to Santa Cruz.

We motored on and on, making stops at Noyo, Shelter Cove, Pt. Arena, Bodega Bay, Drakes Bay, and Pillar Point Harbor. We found Noyo to be very scenic and quaint, although it was one long walk into Fort Bragg. Shelter Cove was definitely inappropriately named. We entered at night and stumbled upon many anchored boats with no anchor lights, and found the anchorage to be very uncomfortable due to rolling. Pt. Arena was fair, but Bodega Bay was great. We anchored outside the harbor although we did go inside for fuel. The outside harbor was very comfortable, but in heavy weather the inside would be preferable. The town was very small and quaint with an excellent waterfront restaurant serving a huge breakfast deliciously cheap! In Bodega we also met our first "disenchanted" world cruisers. It was sad to listen to the couple tell of the time spent in building their boat and outfitting it, only to have their first adventure down the Straits of Juan de Fuca and their run down the Pacific coast totally destroy years of work and dreams of adventure. Added to their predicament, the Coast Guard harassed them mercilessly, going so far as to conduct a late night boarding and search of their vessel. I knew something was amiss when the search party asked for identification from the four of us who'd been chatting aboard their vessel. I didn't have a thing on me and offered to go over to our boat anchored nearby and retrieve my passport. The boarding officer, gun drawn, told me not to bother, nor did he give more than a token glance at Tom's driver's license. He did, however, look over the vessel owner's identification very carefully. After the Coast Guard left, the couple told us that they'd been harassed since they'd anchored because a boat similar in description to theirs was suspected of running drugs. Sure enough, in the morning there the Coast Guard was, slowly circling their sailboat. Shortly afterward, the couple pulled anchor and headed for San Francisco. Later we heard that they'd sold their boat in San Francisco and bought a trailer.

Drakes Bay was also a good anchorage, but like some of the others it would offer little protection in a southerly. Just south of Drakes Bay, refuge from practically any weather can be sought in Pillar Point Harbor.

By the time we reached Pillar Point Harbor we had talked ourselves into wintering in Mexico before leaving for Hawaii. We were in no big rush, and since we'd never seen Mexico but would be so close by the time we got to Southern California, it would be a pity not to take the opportunity of seeing Mexico.

We spent a week in the foggy security of the Pillar Point breakwater anchorage. We went by bus and rapid transit to San Francisco and rode cable cars, trolleys, buses and taxis in our sightseeing and shopping. We bought our charts for Mexico along with home winemaking supplies since we'd been told by several people that wine in Mexico was both terrible and expensive. The man in the brewer's store looked at us in disbelief as we explained that we wanted to make wine on a moving vessel. Not only make it, but drink it soon, for we couldn't afford to let it age a year or more. Tom's plan was to put the bottles in a gimbaled bucket behind the head. That way they would stay "steady" while the wine was fermenting. Ideally we should have begun production three years earlier when we'd left Oregon for Alaska. At a gallon a whack, what with various fermentation stages, we might have had a basic supply built up. The salesman sold us our supplies, somewhat reluctantly, and we left his shop laden with a bucket, book, and numerous little bags of powders and pills.

From Pillar Point we actually sailed, not motored, to Santa Cruz. We had intended on spending a few days there, but we left promptly the next morning after we heard how the bar at Santa Cruz silted in in the fall and boats can be completely landlocked until the bar is dredged the following spring! We sailed across Monterey Bay and spent a week poking about the very picturesque, enticing city. I was sure I kept seeing John Steinbeck at every turn.

Didn't see Mayor Clint Eastwood in Carmel either, but we did anchor in Stillwater Cove off Pebble Beach while we waited for a small southerly to pass. We traipsed along the exclusive golf course and gawked at the fancy houses. Tom went diving and speared huge fish...probably someone's exotic pets. He also found an anchor on the bottom—unfortunately it belonged to another boat nearby.

I swear I saw Patty Hearst in Moro Bay while we spent five days there visiting with Tom's Uncle Charles and Aunt Evelyn. I bought a "lucky" African bean for 39 cents which I could not resist in a gift shop. The beans, supposedly swept along Africa's rivers, or maybe it was the Amazon, are deposited in various places along the coast. Some have been found 1,500 miles away. This bean, which seemed to beckon to me, lives in my magic box with my other treasures twenty odd years after my irresistible urge to pick it up was answered.

From Moro Bay we rounded Point Conception under sail, arriving three hours ahead of our e.t.a. at Santa Barbara. We'd hit an all time high speed of 10.5 knots under jib and reefed main while shooting off a swell, and we'd had an exhilarating sail. The difference between regular six to eight foot running sea to the calm of Southern California waters was very noticeable, and I can understand now why so many Southern Californian sailors are reluctant to head out past Cape Conception, for it is a rude awakening indeed. Past the oil derricks decorated like alien space craft, into a windy stretch, and on to the calm of Santa Barbara we went that night.

Santa Barbara was our first introduction to Southern California, and I'm sure we must have looked like the ogling hicks from the sticks that we were (are). We stared in open disbelief at people on roller skates whizzing up and down the promenade. Totally agog, we watched roller disco in action in the parking lot as participants, bedecked with headphones and elbow and knee pads, pirouetted and leapt about like ballet performers. I could not decide whether I thought it wonderful that people had the opportunity and inclination to explore these new modes of recreation and self-expression, or whether I thought it was decadent and dumb. Oh, my little conservative Oregon self was flabbergasted and incredulous. Farther on were the Frisbee fanatics. Now these people were not just throwing the Frisbee back and forth and chasing it down like one would see on Oregon's college campuses or at the beach. No, they too were performing incredible feats of timing and precision as they'd bump and grind the whirling discs from one part of their body to another, roll it down their backs, up over the shoulders and on to new destinations. The Frisbee had metamorphosed while we'd been more or less lost in the wilderness. As I age I find I appreciate such unbounded pleasure and cavorting much more than when I was young and life was serious. Heck, even I have a tattoo nowadays!

Santa Cruz Island, our next stop, was remarkable in three ways. First, the diving was excellent although a bit cool. The underwater color was incredibly beautiful, and the spear fishing was bountiful. Second, we met up with a boat we'd seen earlier in Oregon (the *Annie-O*) and we met their traveling buddy boat and companions on *Captain James Vashon*. Our paths would cross regularly for the next six months as we all headed into Mexico. Finally, Santa Cruz was remarkable in that it was our first introduction and rude awakening to private property versus cruising. In our years in Alaska we'd never encountered "Private Property" and "Off Limits" islands in the Alaskan archipelago. In Washington and Canada there had never been landing fees or exclusivity—or if there was we were certainly unaware of it. Here we were in the land of "Passes, Permissions, and Privacy." In some respects I can easily understand why a person might not want strangers hiking all over and building campfires on their property. On the other hand, Southern California boaters really have nowhere to go except these islands, and there are so few of them at that. I became convinced that privatization of beaches and other recreational sites is an insult and offense to the tax paying public. It reeks of elitism.

Anyway, we passed from Santa Cruz to Oxnard and then to Santa Monica in search of a wet suit of some sort for me. Santa Monica, home of Marina del Rey, was probably the second most astounding harbor I've ever seen. One could fit all the boats from Alaska and Oregon into the marina and still have room for a lot of Washington's boats too. We were amazed—again we felt like we were from another country, maybe even another planet.

We stayed at the California Yacht Club and were given every courtesy even though when I'd called ahead for a spot the operator asked me three times to repeat our yacht club's name. "The what yacht club?"

"Sauvies Island Yacht Club."

"The who yacht club?"

"Sauvies Island Yacht Club. In Portland, Oregon."

"Where?"

"Portland, Oregon. Willamette River…"

"Come on in and tie up. We'll see what we can do." Laughter in the background.

The dock master was so taken by our audacity to cross an ocean in such a small boat that he went out of his way to help us whenever he could. In fact, our Cal 2-34 did look like a dinghy tender for some of the mammoth vessels moored there. He would come by several times a day and look at us, shake his head, and wish us luck. We were minute compared to the huge racing yachts around us…and we were only two. He loaned us his brand new Toyota one day so we could go get me a wet suit top. Can you imagine two people who hadn't driven in two years in a brand new car in Los Angeles? We were nervous wrecks, with me screaming at every intersection and trying to read off street names in the process.

I had one of my more humiliating experiences going from Oxnard to Marina del Rey. We were motoring along in flat calm when I thought I heard a siren. I went on with my reading, however, and pretty soon looked around for boats. That's when I saw what looked like a big police boat heading towards us. I went back to reading and the next thing I knew there was a siren blasting in my ear. A voice came over a loudspeaker that informed us we were in their missile firing range. I immediately whipped the autopilot off and started steering every which way trying to escape any incoming missiles. I didn't know where to go. The voice spoke again and told me a heading to go on—it was the exact heading we'd been on before I went berserk on the wheel. Sure enough, the area on the chart was marked off limits, but we survived.

I say Marina del Rey was the second most astounding harbor I've ever seen—the first is Newport Beach, in all its rich and astounding splendor. We spent a week in Newport Beach visiting fishing friends from Alaska who winter in Corona del Mar (poor guys) seeing the fantastic Disneyland, and putting about in our skiff, oohing and aahing at the incredible mansions and yachts.

Needless to say, as October dawned we were beginning to get anxious to move on to San Diego, our last top in the United States before we left for Cabo San Lucas in November. Bidding our friends goodbye we left for what was for us the best stop in all of California… beautiful San Diego. Many boaters do not share our enthusiasm for San Diego and point out that the city is incredibly expensive. Well, in a manner of speaking I must agree. San Diego has more boat chandleries located in a small area than any place I've ever seen. And boaters cannot seem to say no to all those little gadgets and devices that they "might" need—the Spare Parts Syndrome all over again—only San Diego is the last chance stop for Mexico bound boaters. Suddenly you find yourself wondering if maybe you shouldn't have a spare gasket set for your engine; well, maybe more fuel filters while you're at it; how about and how about. It can be endless, and of course you don't want to get stranded somewhere in Mexico and have to fly back for parts, so....

We found that almost all of San Diego (then) was an anchorage, although some areas required special permits. We got two 72 hour permits to anchor in Shelter Cove, then we moved to the lovely and accommodating San Diego Yacht Club. We felt we were in the lap of luxury and stayed on for several days after our courtesy moorage expired. We were awaiting money from Alaska and so had an early indoctrination to the money handling problems of travelers. This was, of course, pre debit and ATM card days. The money transfer situation was a problem for us throughout our travels. Some people used their VISA's in traveling and took out cash draws at banks. This might have been a good system although one couple we knew who did this got very frustrated waiting in long lines in Mexican banks. We did use our VISA in Mexico and got charged for things we never purchased...after we'd left the country even. Another boat just had cash mailed to them. I was not that brave, having limited funds. We had our mail opened in the Port Captain's office in Manzanillo and Acapulco and had a pressure cooker gasket removed from an envelope that Tom's mother had sent us. We also never received typewriter ribbons my mother mailed. Actually expecting to receive an envelope full of cash seemed to be wishful thinking to me.

We spent a week in Glorietta Bay at Coronado in San Diego, and it was heavenly. Besides beginning our first batch of wine, each morning we rowed ashore and played tennis, did our exercises, and went running. We did boat projects then, and later we'd take a walk somewhere, or hop on the bus and go downtown. Unbeknownst to us we were in the 72 hour anchorage again, but we stayed six days and no one said anything. We took care of our Mexican paperwork and half jokingly talked about forgetting about spending the winter in Mexico and just spending it there in San Diego. Their October weather was something we'd never before experienced.

Before our departure we moved back to Shelter Island and played the yacht club circuit. We stayed our courtesy nights at each club and then stayed extra and paid for those same number of nights they'd extended to us. We found all the clubs to be hospitable and gracious.

Meanwhile, Tom went crazy again in the marine supply shops, we gulped our share of Baskin-Robbins ice cream, and we ate out often. We spent a lot of time visiting and drinking beer with *Annie-O* and *Captain James Vashon.* We ran every morning and luxuriated in the gorgeous California sunshine. "Well, what do you think the weather is doing in Wrangell right now, Tom?" We'd laugh and kick up our heels feeling so exuberant.

We threw a Bon Voyage party aboard *Cabaret* in which we served some wicked "Alaska Pan-Dowdys". After drinking several you know why "Alaska Pan-Dowdys make your eyes pop out and your stomach say howdy!" We left San Diego October 30th, unable to stand the excitement of our upcoming experience.

SOUTH OF THE BORDER

Our trip from San Diego to Cabo San Lucas would be our longest non-stop passage. We chose to go straight through to see what it was like to be at sea for a long period. Unfortunately the trip was so perfect that it gave us a very distorted image of what passages are like. For one thing, we caught a never ending supply of fresh fish, and the seas were so calm that we were actually able to sit down to three course dinners at night complete with wine…and we didn't have to hold on to our glasses or plates or anything! (Okay, the three course dinner thing is a slight exaggeration since I've never cooked a three course dinner in my life…but you get the idea!) Despite the perfect conditions, we came closer to being run over by a ship on this trip than at any time before or since. (Well, since I slept on most of my watches from Bora Bora to Honolulu this may not be true.) We were careful about keeping night watches, but the daytime found us seeking shade inside, reading and playing games. Very occasionally one of us would peek outside and look around. It just happened that I decided to take a few minutes on deck to check the sails and the autopilot. As I looked forward, what to my wondering eyes should appear, but a humongous freighter bearing directly down upon us—perhaps the

length of a football field away. I emitted a squawk of some sort
as I tried to move my paralyzed legs aft to the wheel. Tom, curious as to why I was floundering about, squawking, waving my arms
frantically, flipping the autopilot off and steering, asked what was
going on. "A ship! Oh my God! A ship! Which way? Which way?"
He came out in a rush at this news. Fortunately, before I began
steering wildly, careening us across the path of the now looming
ship, I noticed it was changing course. I kept my wits for a change
and steered the other direction. We kept a better lookout after this
episode.

The scorching days were followed by cool, damp evenings, so
every night found us bundling up. We ran formal watches of three
hours only at night, commencing at 7:00. By our fourth night out
I was beginning to appreciate what "tired" really meant. We were
also dressing less warmly. By Cedros our sweaters came off; next our
coats were eliminated; sweat shirts followed on the next evening; and
our last night found us stumbling into Cabo San Lucas at midnight
in shorts and t-shirts. It had to be close to 90 degrees. We'd made our
passage in seven days, and here was Cabo!

Cabo of 1980 was a far cry from the condo/hotel/timeshare
conundrum of Cabo nowadays. Cabo then was a dusty, dirty little
Mexican town with one paved road running out of town to a Pemex
station. There were three hotels in those days and perhaps a dozen
cantinas and restaurants. It was quaint, very Mexican, and a refuge
for boats plying the coast.

SO—the famous Cabo: hot, dusty, and expensive, yet somehow
very exciting and foreign. We drank ice cold beer in shady beach
front cantinas admiring the beautiful blue hues of the sea and sky.
It was November and so hot we both got a little sick. Remember,
we'd been declimatized to heat for a long time...like for our whole
lives, what with coming from Oregon and Alaska! I babbled off my
long studied Spanish only to be totally devastated when I understood
not a single word of the reply. This would take more work than I'd
realized, I mused as I looked blank faced at the rapidly talking waiter
before me. I always responded with a simple "Si" and wondered
what had actually transpired. So began a number of unique meals
we were served. Often I had no idea what we were being brought
if the waiter asked to substitute for what I'd ordered, but I always
nodded sagely and said, "Si!" Tom would then ask, "What are we
getting anyway?"

"I don't know," I'd answer, "but it'll probably be okay." This was not Tom's idea of fun, although I found it to be amusing and reminiscent of my days in Europe when I would point to the items on the menu based on their price with no knowledge of what I was getting. Once I was served a bowl of gravy for dinner.

I was also big on insisting that we eat "where the locals eat. It will be really authentic cuisine there, Tom!" This resulted in several meals which Tom disposed of by rapidly and unobtrusively flicking forkfuls of food out the windows and doors. He was good, I must say, because I did not even notice and I was sitting by him stirring my food around, rearranging it so it looked like I'd eaten some of it. The first time he did this I looked in awe at his empty plate, hardly believing my eyes that it was bare, incredulous that he would eat what looked like lard filled tortillas. I happily offered him half of my dinner which he quickly declined. It was not until we left and he headed for a taco stand that I got an inkling of what he'd done. The pack of dogs that had gathered around the restaurant eating his castaways followed him everywhere!

I formulated some life theories in Cabo—ones I still maintain. Theory one: hot weather is not healthful to people who are from temperate climates. For ten months we were subjected to heat that made us occasionally ill. We both lost between ten and fifteen pounds and suffered from bouts of diarrhea. In fact, I don't think the heat is healthful to the locals even, which is probably why the Mexicans and others often take siestas in the heat of the day.

Theory two: nostalgia is deadly. We no sooner arrived in hot, dusty Cabo than Tom began to think Alaska was wonderful. Had I agreed, Tom would have headed *Cabaret* north the day after we arrived. Secretly I was glad he was missing Alaska because then I knew we'd get to go back, but I reasoned that we'd come so far that it would be terrible not to give Mexico a chance and at least see some of it. So at this point we discussed cruising Mexico until May, then off to Hawaii, then home to Alaska. In addition, the more "officialdom" we had to deal with (checking in with port captains and immigration, standing in lines in the heat, etc.) the less we liked it, and the hassle of obtaining ice, fuel, and water bordered on the ridiculous. It was hot; we were cranky.

I remember one particularly pathetic day when Tom went ashore alone to get ice. I refused to accompany him everywhere just because he didn't speak Spanish. I was angry at his dependence on me and angry at having to tramp through heat and dust for fuel and other picayune things. Finally I wrote out in phonetics for Tom all the phrases I thought to be essential:

> *Hay agua por aqui para tomar? (Is there water here to drink?)*
> *Dos cervecas frias. (Two cold beers.)*
> *Dos mas. (Two more)*
> *Hielo, por favor. (Ice please.)*
> *Donde est la sala de bano? (Where is the bathroom?)*

Armed with his little 3×5 index cards Tom rowed ashore for ice. It was only a medium distance for ice, but it was so hot that the ice would always be half melted by the time we'd get back to the skiff. Well, from my shady position under the boom tent, I watched Tom hustling back with two blocks of ice. He got to the landing and, in trying to get everything loaded into our plastic skiff, he slipped on the breakwater and fell, and a block of ice fell into the water. The water in the inner harbor by the breakwater had to be 85 degrees, and there was Tom desperately scrambling trying to retrieve the quickly disappearing ice. Naturally I felt guilty as sin for not helping, and I felt even worse when he finally rowed to the boat, all bloodied and frustrated, with very little remaining ice.

For one week it was so hot we could muster up little more energy than to lie in the shade of our boom tent. Tom became more convinced that Alaska was really paradise—especially after a perilous escape from the breakwater to the dinghy to the head on the boat.

We snorkeled and swam and watched a daily parade of boats arrive. Anchor lines crisscrossed the bottom like highways on a map. It is a wonder that more boats are not lost on the beach there. Most people had (we felt) woefully inadequate anchoring gear, and since they'd spent most of their time tied to a dock or a buoy, they had little experience in setting anchors. The anchorage in Cabo was satisfactory, although a few days we did have a large swell running. The major problem in anchoring there is to make sure your anchor(s) is not fouled by other boaters anchoring over the top. Two anchors were used by most boaters to keep them headed into the swell.

The inner harbor at Cabo was very calm although it was very crowded and dirty. It was much hotter than the outer anchorage since a breeze usually seldom found its way inside. The danger of anchoring inside at that time was the ferry which landed there and turned 360 degrees in the small area upon its departure. We saw a boat, *Toad Hall*, demasted by the ferry when the stern of the ferry hooked onto the boat's anchor line and almost sucked the boat underwater. The rigging of the beautiful 44 foot wooden sloop caught on the upper deck of the ferry and ultimately something had to give...it was not the ferry. The original spruce mast finally gave way with a sickening snap. The ferry did not stop, turn around, or in any way cease its onward progress. The inner harbor in Cabo now has been developed into a beautiful marina lined with hotels, restaurants, and shops.

We left Cabo after ten days of snorkeling and growing fun as we adjusted to the heat and the weather moderated. We were bound for the Sea of Cortez with the intention of returning to Cabo to rendezvous with *Annie-O* and *Captain James Vashon*. Our plan never materialized, however, for the day we headed for Los Frailes the wind was howling down Baja (typical). We pounded away mercilessly and soon asked ourselves why we were suffering when we really didn't need to? We'd spent too many years going to windward under duress to do it now by choice. With that we radioed *Voyager*, a boat we'd met in Cabo who was going with us, and told them we were heading on to San Blas. They concurred, so both of us turned about and suddenly what had been a nightmare became a beautiful 7 knot reach to San Blas.

Thus began our four month trek along the beautiful Mexican coast. Other than the minor trouble of checking in and out of each port with a port captain, we found the trip to be trouble free. We were treated nicely by the Mexican people—or at least if they were rude none of us knew enough Spanish to know that what they were saying was insulting. We ate a steady diet of guacamole, refried beans and tortillas. This was augmented by excellent spear fishing and regularly caught dorado as we slowly advanced from San Blas to Puerto Vallarta.

Even though San Blas has a reputation for being buggy, we did enjoy it. The entrance to San Blas is plenty deep and well marked (1980). The anchorage by the town is small but can easily accommodate half a dozen boats. The river then leads to an immense mangrove swamp which is fun to explore by skiff. Since the bugs only seem to come out at night, it is a good stop as prices on many items seemed reasonable compared to other towns, and the town itself was unspoiled by tourists. Best of all, huge blocks of ice were available at the dock for a trifle. Mantachen Bay, adjacent to San Blas, offered us good anchorage but poor snorkeling. We were treated wonderfully by the inhabitants of the bay after Tom and two other boaters helped a local resident put a new thatched palm roof on his house. Soon a large group of Mexicans were standing about watching the unheard of phenomenon of three Anglos working for a Mexican! Afterwards, these people could not do enough for us; not only did they load us up with fruit, but if we started walking into town they would get up from their meal or whatever they were doing and take us in and would not accept gas money.

We found very good diving at Rincon de Guayabitos where we anchored behind a large island. Later the next day we moved over to the beach and hitchhiked to the small town of La Penita. It was an incredibly clean, quaint little town that was not even on the maps!

We arrived in Banderas Bay for the holiday season, and it proved to be the most culturally diverse Christmas we've ever spent. Where to spend the holiday season in a foreign country can be a difficult decision sometimes, particularly when you've never traveled in the country and are unfamiliar with it. Many boaters we'd met were very specific as to where they wanted to spend the holidays either as a result of previous experience or as a result of recommendations by friends. Most southbound cruisers seemed determined to spend the season either in Las Hadas near Manzanillo, or at the anchorage at Costa Careyes. Quite a large number were planning on flying home for the holidays. A few, like us, were more laissez-faire about the whole holiday scene. We didn't really care where we spent the holidays as long as we'd be able to derive some sort of cultural experience in the process. We wanted to see how Christmas was celebrated in Mexico by Mexicans.

After three hectic weeks in Puerto Vallarta and Guadalajara, however, we were ready to leave the area even though Christmas was still a few days away. The Christmas season in Puerto Vallarta really begins with the celebration of Our Lady of Guadalupe and the holiday atmosphere lasts for weeks We saw the festivities in Puerto Vallarta celebrating Our Lady of Guadalupe: days of parades honoring the miracle of Guadalupe where it is said that the Virgin Mary appeared before a young Mexican named Juan Diego. These parades, colorful with much dancing and singing, contain historical significance regarding the conversion of the various sectors of Mexico to Catholicism. The processions wind down the narrow cobblestone streets and culminate at the entrance to the large cathedral. Afterwards, fiestas and celebrating in the plazas occurs. It is a night out on the town for the local families, and streets and squares jammed with milling people towing children closely behind make quick passageway an impossibility.

Our excursion by bus inland to Guadalajara showed us that it too is a bustle with the holiday spirit and, except for the language spoken, could at first glance be mistaken for any large city in the throes of the holiday rush in the United States. The bus ride from Puerto Vallarta to Guadalajara was an experience in and of itself as Mexico's version of Mario Andretti careened the bus at full speed along the narrow winding mountainous passes. I sat in my seat staring ahead wild eyed murmuring supplication as the driver would pull out and pass on corners that I knew must be the last corner I'd ever see. The scenery, when I could tear my eyes away from the road ahead, was breathtaking according to Tom. I thought I was just breathless from the ride.

Guadalajara is Mexico's craft and cultural center, and we were anxious to visit their Cultural Center, Libertad Market, and Tlaque Paque. We visited all three before we made any purchases so that when we began buying our pottery and weaving we knew what prices were reasonable and what was good quality. It was an exciting week for us and we enjoyed ourselves fully knowing that *Cabaret* was under the watchful eye of George and Diane on *Voyager*. Large downtown malls were decorated with overhanging Christmas décor, window display cases featured Christmas packages beautifully wrapped and set about snow laden plastic trees, and Santa Claus appeared decked out in traditional garbs every few blocks. Our shopping differed only in that we wore t-shirts and sandals and spent meagerly according to the dictates of our cruising budget, as opposed to our northern habits which would have dictated that we bundle up warmly and spend too extravagantly.

On the return trip the bus driver stopped about every two miles to pick up peddlers who boarded the bus to sell their goods. Naturally I sampled everything, including a book on some guru who hated all Americans. The food I tried was tasty, although I sent two young boys into fits of snickers when I bought two tamales and began eating them with the corn wrapper still on.

After two years in the relative isolation of Alaska and eight months cruising, we suddenly found we could not endure another week in Guadalajara or Puerto Vallarta (P.V.) being jostled, bustled, jammed, etc. so we hauled in our anchor and slipped across Banderas Bay to

Yelapa. Before we left we shared our first bottle of Vino Blanco de *Cabaret* with *Annie-O* and *Captain James Vashon* who happened into P.V. where they planned to leave their boats while they flew home for the holidays.

So much has changed in Mexico in the last twenty plus years that I am hesitant to describe the beautiful, picturesque hamlet of Yelapa, some twelve miles from Puerto Vallarta, which looked like a tropical paradise then. It could be a modern suburb as of this writing, but in 1980 it was special. A perfect sandy beach was backed by thatched roof huts and small open cantinas. The hills immediately rose behind, covered with exotic green trees never seen in the Northwest— except on postcards sent by other cruising friends. The town was an interesting walk from the beach in which a stream was to be forded and small mountains scaled. Since Yelapa had no cars it needed no streets—or perhaps it should be the other way around—since it had no streets it needed no cars! Winding dirt and stone trails led us to the city center which had a few small mom'n'pop style food stores, a tortilla making hut, and a ricia factory. Ricia was the local home brew and came in various style bottles and jars. A few restaurants were around, including one called Yelapa Yacht Club. Food, all brought in by boat from Puerto Vallarta, was costly.

The main mode of transportation in this town was feet—human and horse. Many people owned horses and rode them from place to place; some rented horses to visitors and took them on tours. These horses, however, made walking the unlit streets at night a tricky and sometimes slippery business!

The Christmas spirit was in Yelapa too, only on a more subdued and comfortable level. The festivities began on the beach Christmas Eve afternoon when 40 to 50 children gathered about in a circle and took turns swinging a stick at brightly covered piñatas. Shrieks of laughter and screaming ensued in the mad scramble for goodies when a child broke the piñata open. Children would dive fiercely for the candy treasures. Rolling around over the tops of each other and piling on one another gave them and the adult onlookers a great deal of amusement.

All during the afternoon, preparation of hams and turkeys proceeded. Having grown up with Safeway and neatly packaged turkeys, I thought I was interested in seeing the actual process of the butchering and plucking of a turkey. A family was just beginning to prepare to butcher their very large turkey when we were passing by, so

I asked if I could watch. The father, amused by my interest, asked if I might not be afraid. I admitted I was a little nervous but that I really wanted to watch. He carefully explained to his two little girls, and me, what he was going to do. Peeking through my fingers I saw only the first blow, intended to stun the bird, but which served only to set it squawking and flopping about pitifully. I'd had enough. I took off at a sprint amid laughter from other observers.

Not until Christmas Eve were the traditional Christmas decorations brought out, and the scarcity of them made them more precious and appreciated. Families sat down to dinner, church services ensued, and the tiny restaurants filled up for a candlelight repast. Later a highly anticipated dance was put on to which the local people came dressed in their finest. A festive evening followed, complete with dancing, beer, and loud scratched up records. Elaborately decorated, the dance hall was filled to capacity with onlookers standing outside enjoying the mild weather and cold beer. We left at 1:00 A.M, but the party was only just getting into full swing.

Christmas Day was the most unusual Christmas we'd ever spent. After 30 Christmases in the Northwest, ranging from Oregon to Alaska, this was our first Christmas without rain, snow, cold weather or all three. We snorkeled in the warm water of Banderas Bay and kept wondering what kind of weather our families were having for the holidays. Of course we generally knew what the weather at home would be like, but we wanted details so we could gloat.

For Christmas dinner we gathered for a stupendous four boat potluck, complete with ham, sweet potatoes, salad, rice, fish casserole, refried beans, chocolate cake, pumpkin pie and homemade bread. The fare was more elaborate than we'd eaten in many months. Basically strangers before, we spent our Christmas together, sharing our food, memories, and boating yarns: Howard, Jeff, and Karen on *Sea Bear*, Al and Peggy on *Gi Gi*; George and Diane on *Voyager*, and us on *Cabaret*. We said goodnight as the cool land breeze sprang up and we returned to *Cabaret* to reflect on a most unique Christmas.

Three days later the surf picked up making dinghy landings almost impossible, so we tore ourselves away from Yelapa and Banderas Bay and began again our meandering pilgrimage south. From Yelapa we ducked around the corner to the tiny towns of Ipala and Antigua. The poverty there put a damper on our enjoyment of them. While the children were curious and friendly, the adults stared glumly out of their gloomy makeshift stick houses.

In the center of the small stick housing complex in Antigua was a very large communal garbage dump with literally hundreds of old beer cans. The beach where we landed our skiff was littered with the remains of turtle carcasses. Overall, squalor and poverty reigned. The town of Ipala, a short distance away, was better cared for and organized where pick-ups served as shuttle buses for the people carrying them between the two towns. Both days that we were anchored, we were visited by boatloads of young swimmers who smiled shyly and giggled at my Spanish. Uncomfortable at the blatant disparity between our lifestyle and that of the pescadores living in the stick shacks ashore, we soon left for Chamela, a large bay with good anchorage, and thence to one of our favorite stops, Careyes, where we spent New Years.

The Hotel Careyes, at that time very hospitable to boaters, is tucked away inside a tiny trio of coves. It is not a good anchorage in a southerly or westerly, but we were securely hidden behind a rock island and were very comfortable. We spent ten wonderful days there diving in neighboring coves and enjoying the use of the hotel's free showers. Nightly we'd swim ashore towing the dinghy, and after a luxurious hot shower we'd retire to the bar for our spendy drinks. We hitched into the town of Chamela quite a few miles distant where there was a Conasuper (market) and we could load up on food supplies. The News Years fireworks at Careyes were sensational. We were amazed at the ingenuity, sheer size, and originality of the Mexican firework display.

Our next stop, Tenacatita, was an excellent anchorage and the diving was good. Again we journeyed by skiff through the small mangrove waterway that feeds into the bay. Our next big leap—all of six miles—was Bahia de Navedad. The anchorage there was also good, and the town of San Patricio made for interesting walks and shopping. At the southern end of Bahia de Navedad is the town of Barre de Navedad, small but affluent in comparison to San Patricio. While we were there Barre de Navedad was holding its annual world swordfish derby. The weather turned ugly, however, and I don't think anyone caught one.

We spent eight days in Bahia de Navedad, stormed in mostly, in one of the most intense storms we'd yet anchored in. The wind swept us in full 360 degree circles, and the rain was like a solid wall. Once the wind ceased we put out our rain catcher and completely filled our water tanks in a few hours. Our skiff also filled, however, and we found ourselves in the middle of the night on deck in the torrential rains trying to raise a skiff gunnel deep in water. We were lucky not to lose the skiff or injure ourselves hoisting the heavy, waterlogged thing aboard.

We anchored in Manzanillo for two days in front of the highly touted Las Hadas before we moved to Manzanillo proper. Built like a sultan's mecca and immortalized by the move "10", Las Hadas seemed to offer privacy only at a very high price. Although we had been warned away from Manzanillo by other boaters, we enjoyed our brief stop there. Manzanillo itself is a bustling city with one of the greatest bars (then) in all of Mexico—The Bar Social. From about 1:00 P.M. on hors d'oeuvres at about 5 pesos a plate are served nonstop along with ice cold beer. Literally plates and plates of tostadas, guacamole, bean dip, cerviche, and tacos were available. You are served as much as you like in what was one of the more captivating and clean establishments we'd been in. Twice an afternoon a raffle took place for chickens, and sometimes a three piece, old timer band provided music. The atmosphere, food, clientele, and lack of décor was all but perfect.

It was here, in Manzanillo, that we decided to forego the May passage to Hawaii and to go on to Costa Rica and Panama—after all we were so close, we reasoned, we should take advantage of our proximity. What we would do or where we would go after Panama was a good question, but one we figured we'd answer when the time came. And when we met Kent and Caroline Barber at Las Hadas who had decided to return to San Francisco for the time being rather than go on to the Caribbean and had all the necessary charts which we needed and they were willing to sell, we felt our fate was ordained. Gleefully we bought charts from them and went back to the boat to celebrate our new destination.

Zihuatenejo, our next stop, is what many boaters think of as the ultimate in Mexican ports. Clean and quaint, the town of Zihuatenejo (called Zihuat by most boaters) offers secure anchorage in the large bay. Block ice and pop are delivered to the stone wharf daily for the restaurant owners across the bay who pick up the goods in their pangas. The merchants were willing to sell ice to boaters, so for a brief interlude we again enjoyed ice cold beverages. The diving in Zihuat was disappointing, however, due to the water being so murky from the recent unsettled weather, but we still enjoyed the warm water for swimming. Many boaters we met spent literally months at anchor in Zihuat; we found ten days was our limit just about anywhere, and so after a brief excursion to Isla Grande for an afternoon of snorkeling, we headed on for our last Mexican port of call: Acapulco.

We were prepared to hate Acapulco, but when we left three and a half weeks later we had to admit it was definitely worth a return visit some time in the future. We stayed at the Acapulco Yacht Club, a treat for us after months at anchor, and I highly recommend this to other boaters. The price (1980 was .25 a foot a day) was cheap insurance against the theft that occurs on boats left at anchor. (While we were at the yacht club no theft occurred to anchored boats to our knowledge, although pickpockets were working the bus routes.)

My mother and aunt joined us for a week in Acapulco, and we had a wonderful time showing them around the town and lounging by the yacht club pool. We ate out nightly and became regular customers at Papa Diaz restaurant nearby. We took my relatives shopping, and Tom helped my aunt barter for her gifts even though she, like me, tended to pay whatever was asked. My mother, however, drove the salesmen nuts when she would walk out of their stalls if they would not meet her low price. At one point we had a small army of salesmen following us arguing and shouting at her. They finally gave in and she got her bargains. I was both impressed and embarrassed. Perhaps one of the reasons why Acapulco was my favorite stop was because of my family's visit and the fun we had together.

Acapulco was also a workstop for us, for at this point we decided once and for all that we were off to the Marquesas next and were not going to Costa Rica and Panama as earlier planned. By Acapulco we were tired of coastal cruising and ready for the big jump: an ocean passage. We had just harbor hopped from Sitka, Alaska, down the entire length of the North American continent and were ready for a change. So our stay found us working madly in the morning hours and lounging comfortably by the yacht club pool in the afternoons. A trip into town to get parts or other items was an all morning affair what with the buses, so it's not like we really were overworked, but we were more focused than we'd been in a long time. Tom also took the time to rebuild a small diesel engine for a fellow boater who was stranded. They dismantled the small engine and laid it out piecemeal in the cockpit. Tom sent the owner back to Los Angeles with a list of parts and tools that he needed to rebuild the engine. Three days after the parts were carried back in luggage, the engine was reassembled and the owner was underway, but without his wife who had to fly back to Los Angeles hurriedly since she had developed hepatitis from helping out sick boaters in Nicaragua where they'd all been held captive at gunpoint for weeks. They had an exciting tale to tell which didn't make me feel one bit sad about skipping Costa Rica and Panama.

I think we also enjoyed Acapulco so much because we finally said to hell with budgeting and spent money exactly (well, almost exactly) as we wanted. We ate out regularly, did all the sightseeing we wanted, and in general acted like real tourists. Regrettably many boaters are on budgets like we were, and I will say that I do think boaters miss out on a lot due to trying to get so far on so little. We were not pleased with traveling with such limitations, and in Acapulco we decided to travel the way we wanted to even if it meant we went shorter distance. Basically we traded quantity for quality and for us it was the best trade, for by Acapulco we knew we would never be world cruisers, especially Tom. We had been gone from Alaska only ten months, but we were often restless and fidgety. Our daily regime of snorkeling and exploring was no longer the perpetually satisfying activity we had once imagined them to be. Granted, we read voluminously and maintained a daily exercise routine, but still we felt stifled. Many boaters do not at all suffer this malaise and seem to adapt to their retirement readily, but we both found ourselves asking, "Is this all? Is this what cruising is about?" We were screaming for activity. No matter how many hours we spent analyzing the problem, we could find no answer to our restlessness. Tom particularly suffered, and often he tore things apart on the boat to have something to do in putting it back together... better. Other cruisers seemed to be content to spend days upon days puttering around their boats and reading. We knew people who spent months in one bay—ten days was our absolute maximum.

So, in Acapulco we decided to head for the Marquesas, Tuomotus, Societies, and end up in Hawaii. With great anticipation we made lists of chores to do and items to buy. My mother brought us our charts when she came. We assured her that the trip would be a piece of cake. Little did I understand then the worry of a mother.

Three days before our departure who should appear but *Annie-O* and *Captain James Vashon*. We enjoyed their company before we left, and our send off from the yacht club was one we'll never forget. We wondered how long it would be before we saw these wonderful people again.

And yes, between his 3×5 cards and his hitherto unknown flair for charades, Tom communicated beautifully in Spanish by the time we left!

BUTT-HIKING IN
POLYNESIA

WELL, YOU KNOW ALREADY that the "no-big-deal-piece-of cake" crossing was anything but that. We were badly bruised psychically, but we had survived. I tended to remember more of the good times of the trip—the spectacular sunrises and sunsets, the incredibly clean air, the flying fish, the sound of the water hissing quietly along the hull, the whole novelty of what we were doing. Tom was a bit more focused on the negative aspects of the trip: the storms, the tedium, the inching across the charts, the exhaustion, and the bad food I cooked. I tended to forget those things because, quite frankly, it was just too scary to remember.

We had both read Robert Suggs's excellent book, *Hidden Worlds of Polynesia*, while enroute to the Marquesas. The book, an archeological study of Nuku Hiva, provided excellent background and really enhanced our enjoyment of what we saw. It gave us a better understanding of the Marquesan people and the way of life they abandoned.

We were warmly greeted by Larry and Leslie Debus from the *Shannon Marie* upon our arrival. They brought us ice cold beers and tuna sandwiches. It had been so rough and I'd been so tired that we'd eaten nothing for three days but cornmeal mush or brown rice with sugar and milk, so the sandwiches and beer hit the spot. When we rowed ashore we were amazed to see a thick patch of goosenecks along the side of our hull! We'd thought fiberglass was immune to growth of that sort, particularly when the boat had been moving through the water. The goosenecks had adhered to the starboard quarter and were half way up the hull. We got them off later by using a pancake scraper. As we looked around we noticed we weren't the only fiberglass boat with above waterline growth!

We stayed a total of seventeen days at Taioha Bay, partly for recuperation psychologically and physically, and partly because the trades were howling and we could not face the prospect of going out into them. Our seventeen days were spent enjoyably, however, and we began slowly to get back into shape after a month of atrophying. After spending at least an hour or two every day trying to ferret out fresh vegetables which we were both craving, we took long walks into the valleys in the bay and looked for ancient stone tikis and temple platforms. The valleys, once highly populated, are now nearly bereft of people, but the steamy tropical appearance of the area makes one feel that primitive people are still scurrying through the underbrush watching one's progress. The greenery was lush and dense, and we were told by the banker that the old Marquesans were saying that it had been thirty years since they'd seen the island so green. He also told us that for the last three years there'd been no dry season as such. I can believe it, for we got rain at least once daily—sometimes in the form of fierce squalls, and I was so glad to be at anchor chasing down my flapping laundry near land instead of at sea. Our walks were hot, sticky and bug-ridden. No-nos and mosquitoes were a constant irritation, and no matter what type of anti-bug repellant we put on, we still got bitten. We even bought a small jar of Tiger Balm, a Chinese product for bites. I only know it smelled so good I had a hard time keeping from trying a mouthful.

Unfortunately, swimming and diving in Taihoa Bay was not recommended due to the terribly high incidence of staph infection. We saw boaters who were covered with hideous, weeping sores. Even the Marquesans often had horrible scars on their legs and ankles from past sores. I'd never seen anything quite like it, and we were appalled at the condition some of the boaters and the Marquesans were in. One couple whom we met later told us that when they were in Fiji they could tell with almost 100% accuracy which boaters had spent time in the Marquesas by the scars on their legs. We got off scar free due to Dr. Tom's protective measures! First, we did not swim in the bay; second, we bathed at least once daily with fresh water and soap in the concrete shower stall ashore. Many boaters seemed to think that just diving into the water several times a day takes care of bathing. This does not clean the skin like fresh water and soap. Third, we treated all cuts and scratches immediately with fresh lime juice—it smarted but it seemed to cauterize the wound. We tried (in vain) not to scratch bug bites, but I had a particularly difficult time of it since I get bug bites one hundred to one to Tom's. My feet and ankles were bitten so badly that every night once they got too warm under the sheet, I'd end up having to get up, bathe my feet in cold, fresh water, smear them with calamine lotion, and then try to sleep with them elevated. Neither of us got open wounds or developed scars from sores or bites, but it took constant vigilance. We found that the least minor scrape flared up and was difficult to cure.

We checked in with the gendarmes and were told we'd have to pay a bond to be able to stay there. We knew this in advance, though, but had hoped we could write either a personal check or use VISA. We were told we could only do this in Tahiti. So we wired home for money to be sent to us in care of the Bank of Indo-Suez in Papeete for us on *Cabaret* in Nuku Hiva. Amazingly within four days the whole transaction was completed with no fuss or muss. I couldn't imagine accomplishing the same task in Mexico. The officials with whom we dealt were courteous, efficient, friendly, and most patiently endured my high school French.

Some Europeans refused to pay the bond because they said they were members of the (then) Common Market and shouldn't have to pay. The French did nothing to them. Other people said they'd pay in Tahiti, and they were given clearance to go to Tahiti without paying. One boat we met never did pay anything and spent six months cruising Polynesia. They were never stopped, questioned, or in any way bothered, nor did they bother to stop and check in with the local gendarmes! See what you get for following the rules?

Nuku Hiva is well known for its wood carvers, and so one afternoon Tom and I sought out Mano, an old man whose fingers were gnarled by arthritis. Mano agreed to make two wooden tikis for us out of Toa wood for the cost of 2,000 francs each ($20.00 in 1981). We gave him $2.00 down and were told to return in four days. Four days later, however, Mano had not yet finished even the first tiki. We told him we were going to another bay but would return in a week or so and would pick them up then. Mano wanted a cash advance, however, and asked me to pay in advance for them. Aha! My "civilized" mind could foresee problems. I refused to pay for both but reluctantly agreed to pay for the one he was working on and had almost completed. I told him I'd pay for the other upon its completion. He agreed to this and so I paid and left, without receipt or any evidence of paying. A week later when we returned for the carvings, Mano not only remembered I'd paid for the first, but also remembered the $2.00 deposit which I'd completely forgotten about. Our transaction was speedily and happily concluded, and I wondered why all business dealings could not be conducted so easily and honestly. I felt a little sheepish about not having trusted him.

While in Taioha we were lucky to see a Marquesan celebration complete with ancient dances. The celebration was a political dinner, and the dances were included as part of the festivities. The ancient pig dance was performed first, followed by a number of hip twisting, gyrating dances in Marquesan costume. It was an interesting evening and yet it was sad to see these people performing dances that had once been an integral and colorful part of their lives. How much longer would they be remembered?

One of our excursions on Nuku Hiva took us to Tai Oa Bay, also locally called Daniel's Bay because of the very famous and excellent woodcarver who lived there. Tai Oa valley, once with 4,000 people living in it, was inhabited only by five people when we visited: Daniel and his wife, Antoinette; Francois and Elaine, Daniel's relatives and the ancient chief we never saw. We anchored there for several days and had a number of unusual experiences.

One day Francois and Elaine acted as our tour guides and took us and several other boaters on a hike to the world's second tallest waterfall. (We were told that statistic by a British couple.) The hike was a long, grueling walk through steamy jungles with the promise of a nice swim at the end. For some reason almost everyone took off at a charge of the light brigade pace with Francois, storming through the jungle like Green Berets on a mission. Mercifully Tom stayed back with Shannon, Leslie and me, three of the most hapless hikers Elaine had probably ever led on a hike. It was a good thing he remained. We slipped, slid, and stumbled along the jungle route, falling in the streams we had to cross and sliding down muddy embankments. He pulled us across one stream, half carrying all three of us at the same time after he'd caught Shannon, a tiny five foot muppet, as she'd been swept downstream after slipping in the fast current. Leslie—aristocratic, sophisticated and willowy—dressed in her yacht whites (which would never be white again) could stumble over a pebble in the path—and often did. Then there I was, dressed like Nanook of the North to keep from being devoured by bugs but being devoured anyway, being my overly cautious, clumsy self. We had a gay old time, slipping, sliding, and laughing. From our appearance, one could not help but wonder if we'd simply skid all over Nuku Hiva on our butts. Our clothes were wet and mud soaked. Leslie proposed an article to be called "Butt Hiking in Polynesia." I promised her then it would be the chapter title of a book.

Elaine stopped often in the course of the walk and pointed out several things of historical interest. One was an ancient poi pit, probably 300 years old. The people would put their breadfruit in these pits and let it ferment into a paste-like substance. The other historical item was a casket set high up on the ledge of a very steep, sheer-sided mountain. Supposedly a king's son was entombed in the casket which sat on a ledge of the mountain. How the ancient people ever dragged the casket up there was beyond my speculation. We also saw ancient stone tikis and many ancient stone platforms. Later, four of us went exploring on our own and found a burial pit in one of the stone heaps. We found what looked like femur and shin bones (and an old bullet). We knew Robert Suggs would be quite jealous of our find! We replaced the bones carefully since they tended to want to disintegrate upon being touched. I was afraid of contracting the Curse of the Leg Bone.

The waterfall and pool for swimming was spectacular, and the water was cold too! Most of us went in for a swim, but Francois and Elaine didn't. They said the water was too cold for them. Some of the boaters went swimming nude. We found it interesting that the French, who taught the natives to wear clothing and considered them barbaric and heathen for going without, were the first boaters to run about completely naked. In every bay was a group of French boaters who paraded about in the buff, oblivious of their own colo-nizing rules and anybody else. I have always been of the belief that most people look better with clothes on than off, myself included, so it was easy for me to refrain from the swim.

Upon our return from the hike Daniel and his wife treated all of us to a delicious roast pig, baked in a pit along with bananas, rice and coconut milk. The brains were considered a great delicacy, and fortunately they did not offer us any, but instead removed them to be eaten by themselves later on. I was so happy about that! It was an excellent meal, and for the first time I tasted roast pork that made me want seconds…and thirds. After dinner we played a game on their front lawn. It was like a Sunday meal with the family—except we spoke in broken French and English and were in another hemisphere.

Loaded with stalks of bananas and several dozen pompomoose, breadfruit and pomegranates, we pitched and crashed our way back to Taioha Bay where we provisioned the boat (at great expense) and prepared to head to the other islands. Unfortunately, Up Pu was inaccessible due to heavy swells in the bay, so we headed on for Hiva Oa via Tahuata.

Throughout our stay in Nuku Hiva we had regularly called for Helen and Elmer Olson on *Elysium* on the radio since we knew they were enroute to the Marquesas from Panama. We figured we'd probably missed them, however, especially when we heard how some boats took upwards of fifty days to cross from Panama. So when we left Nuku Hiva behind us I also felt we'd left our one chance to see these friends. It was too bad, really, but the odds of our finding them were very remote, especially when they didn't know we were looking for them. But what should appear before our eyes as we slowly advanced towards Hana Moe Noe but the familiar mast of *Elysium*. "Is it them, Tom?" I anxiously asked.

"It sure looks like 'em!" And it was.

As we motored in to set anchor Elmer apparently looked out the porthole and calmly said, "That looks like Tom and Becky."

"Nonsense, Elmer. What would they be doing here? They're in Mexico." Helen responded. "My God! It's them!" And so began our long awaited reunion. We spent several days with them diving in the clear water of Hana Moe Noe and talking our fool heads off. They had landed at Hiva Oa and were headed to Nuku Hiva. As it turned out we almost missed them entirely since they'd planned on leaving the night we arrived, and we'd almost gone to Hana Menu instead of Hana Moe Noe. We talked over the old times on Sauvies Island and compared passages. They'd crossed from the Galapagos to Hiva Oa in 26 days and had to hand steer for 23 of those days when their autopilot broke. We both agreed that the little arrows indicating winds of Force 3 and 4 were a figment of someone's imagination. It is remarkable that all cruisers we have talked with share our same feelings!

Helen showed us her incredible collection of shells and fed us her delicious homemade cinnamon rolls. We ate cinnamon rolls regularly after that and actively began to collect shells also. Before, it had been a hit or miss proposition for us, but after seeing Helen's amazing collection we collected in earnest. Unable to talk them into going to Fatu Hiva with us, we reluctantly said goodbye and went our separate ways. Our paths never again crossed in Polynesia, and yet we were all on the lookout for each other.

Hiva Oa was a pleasant stop for us, even so we only stayed three days. The village was about a two mile walk from the harbor, but the local residents seemed very willing to offer rides. We hiked one day to a farm where we went wild buying a watermelon, cantaloupe, pineapples, cucumbers, bananas, and a liter of fresh honey. The hike there was bad going since it was all uphill, but the return was easy. But no matter how hard we tried, we could get no diesel in Hiva Oa, which meant we had only the twenty gallons we'd picked up in Nuku Hiva to get us all the way to Tahiti—a distance of only a thousand miles, but one which we believed could have a lot of calms. Foolish worry.

We left Hiva Oa after Easter Sunday services and headed for Fatu Hiva. We attended local church services regularly in Polynesia I might add, largely because I started feeling a sudden religious revival after our last crossing knowing we had two more to go. A couple of times we did not know what denomination the church was, nor did we understand any of the services since they were usually conducted in the local dialect or rapid French, but we found the Polynesian singing extremely robust, beautiful, and inspirational. The people took a curious interest in us; often we were the only foreigners at the services, so we were regarded with furtive, questioning glances.

We had a lazy, slow sail to Fatu Hiva, but we didn't complain because we were glad to have a beam reach instead of a hard beat like we'd had in going from Nuku Hiva to Tahuata. Since it was my birthday, Tom baked me a Mud Bottom cake and a peach cobbler. We ate them both immediately and speculated that this was probably the most exotic birthday I would ever have. "How many people celebrate their thirty-third birthday while sailing into Nuku Hiva eating Mud Bottom cake and peach cobbler?" Tom asked.

"You're right, Tom. This is great! What will you plan for me next year?"

Twelve hours later, at midnight, we reached Hana Vave on Fatu Hiva, a 35 mile trip from Hiva Oa. With the aid of *Shannon Marie's* anchor light and the beams of a white full moon we entered this beautiful and famous bay.

If I had thought Nuku Hiva was primitive, I was really in for an eyeful in Fatu Hiva. Hana Vave is a small bay—not particularly good anchorage due to poor holding ground in part of it—with no stores of any kind. A small settlement of people live there whose chief occupation seemed to be trading fresh fruit for various goods from visiting boaters. It was really disappointing in some ways to have teenagers meet us at the beach demanding disco tapes in exchange for oranges and bananas. T-shirts and pierced earrings were other big trading items, as were hats, perfume, lipstick, and bras. In some ways one cannot blame the people for wanting these items, after all they are popular items in the United States also, and if it was not for trading, they really had no other means of easily obtaining them. Nevertheless, I guess I was surprised and, probably wrongfully, a little disappointed.

Fatu Hiva is most known, of course, for Thor Heyerdahl's fascinating book, *Fatu Hiva*, in which he several times brings up the people's cannibalistic past, their syphilis, and elephantiasis. This, of course, does not particularly endear Thor to the local people who felt he overemphasized their cannibalism. Robert Suggs also said the Nuku Hivans were cannibalistic, but that their dietary anomaly was only a periodic celebratory activity to mark a victory over an enemy. This impressed us, particularly when we saw how big the Nuku Hivans were! Cannibalism has not been practiced in at least 100 years, and most probably longer. While it was true that elephantiasis was apparent among some of the older Marquesans for we ourselves saw some cases, the younger people do not seem to be afflicted with this disease due to preventative medicine. In fact, elephantiasis has all but been eradicated among the Tuomotus and Society Islands, with only a small number of cases still in the Marquesas. My three dread diseases were elephantiasis, leprosy and rabies, so I was very apprehensive about contracting either of the first two while we were in the Marquesas. (These diseases have been replaced by Mad Cow Disease, rabies, leprosy, and flesh eating bacteria.) I was told, however, that in the most remote, one-in-a-million chance that I contracted elephantiasis, all I had to do was return to my native climate and the cold weather would make it dormant. That was somewhat of a relief (but I wondered what people from Arizona or Florida would do.) And finally, if the people were syphilitic, as Thor Heyerdahl said, they had only the white man to thank for that.

We stayed in Hana Vave a week, visiting with *Shannon Marie*, *Sumitra* and *Starlight*, owned by Mike Davidson, a member of our yacht club. We swam daily, although I'm not sure that Hana Vave was a good bay for swimming since raw sewage ran into the bay along the beach, and we went on hikes with Larry and Leslie Debus from *Shannon Marie*. Again we found a waterfall, not the world's tallest, but probably the world's most hidden. We'd set out for it the day before, but wrong turn led to wrong turn, and we'd had to return in a hot sticky torpor to our boats. The following day, Augustine, a friendly local resident, led us to the falls where we enjoyed a refreshing swim.

Another day we were invited to travel aboard the *Shannon Marie* to the next bay, Omoa. We gladly accepted the invitation and set off early in the morning for our visit to Omoa, a regular metropolis compared to Hana Vave. There all of us bought a tapa, an art form for which Fatu Hiva is well known. We were told by another boater that the tapas in Fatu Hiva were the best in all of the South Pacific. The tapa is made from the bark of the breadfruit tree. It is pounded until it is paper thin and then it is left in the sun to dry. Finally, it is pounded again and traditional native designs are drawn or painted on the cloth. I was so happy to buy a tapa, but not quite sure exactly what I'd do with it once I got it home.

After a week, we loaded up with oranges, pompomoose and bananas and took final leave of the Marquesas. They were, and are, still enthralling to me. I was glad to have the opportunity to visit them before "civilization" completely overwhelmed them (complete with tour ships and an international airport.) Whether or not the Marquesans have benefited from "civilization" is debatable. Naturally, one can point to the medical care they now receive and to their schooling. But really one can also see so many negative aspects. Introduction to western canned foods and processed sugar has not improved their health. The average Marquesan appears overweight and dental education must be almost nil since many seemed to be missing teeth. And what of their own culture do they have left? Of course all cultures must change, but one cannot help but feel the Marquesan change was not gradual—nor was it particularly wanted.

LOST IN THE
TUOMOTOS

WE LEFT HANA VAVE on Fatu Hiva April
25th, 1981. In some ways I was reluctant to leave because the
Marquesas had been so totally unique for me. The people, the jungles,
and way of life were absolutely unlike anything I'd ever seen. I had
been fascinated by the tropical islands and would have liked to have
done more hiking and exploring had the heat not been so forbid-
ding. I watched the weight melt off Tom—and he had none to spare
in those days. Actually I think the Marquesas were the first place
I "got into" sweat, since sweating felt so good in the intense, prickly
heat of the jungle islands.

My big mistake in going from the Marquesas to the Tuomotos
was to underestimate the distance…a mere 600 miles I thought to
myself as I perused the charts…no time at all. Hot, windless conditions slowed us considerably the first two days (remember we had
only twenty gallons of fuel to get us about 1,000 miles.) So we poked
along for four light wind or calm days and nights with occasional
small squalls moving us a few "bonus" miles. Our fifth day was very
squally and we were unable to get an MP. Our log indicated we'd
run 90 miles, but for some reason we both felt we'd gone much farther. That night we were in a series of hideous squalls with rain so
hard I literally could not see the back of the boat from the back of

119

the boat. We decided to heave to due to such heavy weather, our basically uncertain position, and my refusal to stand my watch. I was actually worried about drowning from just trying to breathe.

The next day our real troubles began. We motor sailed most all day with the squalls gradually diminishing. Tom miraculously managed to get an MP of 144.33W and 14.24S after I threw a small tantrum because of the difficulty in trying to shoot with the boat pitching about madly. Somehow, however, he plotted the position wrong, so we thought we'd drifted past Takaroa at night and then had continued sailing past it all day. Fortunately at 3:00 that afternoon we discovered our true position and we were only twenty miles east of Takaroa's southern end. We kept motor-sailing hoping we'd make it by dark since we were tired from the squalls of the previous day and night. From the Log of the *Cabaret:*

May 1, 1981

Well…we are still trying to find our way to Takaroa. At this point I am so depressed I can't stand it. Got an excellent sunshot, so we headed for Takaroa—but it wasn't there! How about that. The RDF is picking up beacons, but since we don't know the letters for the stations it does us no good. Weather overcast and squally again today.

MP today put us at 144.44 W and 14.13 S. But Takaroa is still sight unseen.

We hove to last night. Tonight we will charge on in the darkness and hope we don't go aground.

We didn't charge on, and since it clouded up and rained that evening Tom got off no star shots. We decided to drift all night rather than run toward reefs in the pitch black. Currents in the Tuomotus are largely unpredictable and sometimes very swift. We had no idea how far we drifted that night, but at first light we set sail in the direction of where we thought Takaroa to be.

At noon on May 2, I got another perfect MP—now it showed us far south of Takaroa. Fortunately we'd only made about fifteen miles that day (by the log) due to such light winds, so we altered course once again. I cried. Frustration, fatigue, shortage of fuel, the heat, and just plain worry got the better of me. I cried over my failure as a navigator, and I cried because I knew we were lost and would be floundering forever. Besides that, I felt like it.

Later we took turns jumping overboard and being dragged by the boat through the warm water, and we made up songs about our gastrointestinal reaction to pompomoose and banana diets. Finally, at 5:00 that evening Tom spotted Takaroa and Takapoto from his rope ladder to the spreaders. We motor-sailed full speed to make it before dark, but once again had to drift that night, but at least we had the lights of Takaroa in view…until they turned them off at midnight.

I'm glad our first coral atoll was a small, sparsely populated one. It was an incredible experience to see that yes, atolls actually do look just like the pictures in elementary school geography text books! Takaroa's entrance to the lagoon was a good reminder of the rapids running we had done in Canada, but once inside the lagoon it was like nothing we'd ever experienced.

Shannon Marie showed up (they'd had their share of troubles locating the atoll also, so I felt better) so we anchored in a small shallow protected area of the lagoon and began a week of exploration and snorkeling with the sharks.

We saw firsthand that week why the Tuomotus were called the Graveyard of the Pacific by boaters. On Takaroa's reefs rested the remains of several large vessels—one a 296' schooner, and the other a Japanese steel fishing boat. I figured that if the fishing boat with radar ran ashore, then it would stand to reason that a lot of boats without radar would probably do the same. We personally know of three cruising boats that were lost in the Tuomotos—all three went aground while traveling at night with no one on watch; all three were total losses. (You know that bond we had to pay when we arrived in Nuku Hiva? That bond covers airfare back to the United States.) One vessel belonging to a friend went aground on a radioactive reef in the French nuclear bombing test zone. He was enroute from Pitcairn Island to Tahiti. A veering of the wind that night when he'd dropped off to sleep in exhaustion set his small sturdy craft solidly aground. With breakers flooding and tearing at the floundering craft, he was able to send off an S.O.S. on his ham radio. The signal was picked up by a ham operator in Australia who contacted French authorities. Our friend and his son were airlifted off the reef, questioned extensively and then released. The boat and its contents remained.

Another couple ran hard aground and lost their beautiful 60 foot craft and years of labor building her. They walked away with their lives and the clothes on their backs. The stories can go on and on, and the atolls themselves each bear the visible remains of all those dreams that came to such an abrupt end.

The 296 foot schooner we explored had been "hurled" ashore in a hurricane—the only one the area has supposedly ever had. Larry and Leslie hiked with us to these wrecks, and the shimmering heat on the windless side of the atoll was more than any of us could bear. After looking through the wrecks we headed back to our boats via the lagoon side of the atoll. Happily a local native in a small skiff gave us a ride to our skiff some miles yet distant.

Our snorkeling adventures were another matter. We saw sharks, and lots of them. The locals told us not to worry, sharks inside the lagoon were harmless, only ones outside were dangerous. I remained skeptical of this local folklore and pretty terrified whenever I saw those big, gray bodies silently gliding by eyeballing me maliciously. Naturally I would start flailing and hyperventilating trying to yell with my snorkel in my mouth whenever I'd see one. Our first near-shark experience was the best, however.

The four of us had gone over to a coral head near our boat in our Avon. We all piled out of the Avon and took off, with Tom leading, followed by Leslie, Larry, and then the chicken of the sea, me. Tom dove and was some 20 feet down and swimming along when I noticed him begin to back pedal and surface. Instantly upon his surfacing I saw Leslie grab him and duck behind him. As I edged closer to Larry the reason for Leslie's maneuvers was clear, for directly below and behind Tom had been a huge, six-foot whitetip shark. Yikes! I grabbed Larry and almost drowned him trying to walk on water to the coral head nearby. And now there was not just one shark slowly circling, but three, four, six, hundreds for all I knew. We beat a hasty retreat to the skiff after fifteen minutes of trying to ignore them like the locals had instructed us.

We spent several more days at Takaroa, diving, trying to develop an insatiable craving for hearts of palm since the people off *Galadriel* were hacking the hell out of the palms trying to get a supply set up, and in poking about the small settlement. I bought some interesting shell necklaces…mostly because the price was so low I couldn't say no, and we visited with other boaters. We signed our names in Takaroa's yacht book and were really proud to do so since we were in their first book.

We left Takaroa, my first atoll and one I'll never forget, for Rangiroa, one of the bigger atolls in the island chain. We arrived off Rangiroa about midnight the following night after we left Takaroa. It was a lousy night for visibility, so we hove to after we made contact with some lights. We were perhaps a ½ to ¼ mile from the atoll and could not see it even though we knew it had to be there. Such is visual navigation in the Tuomotos! One cannot afford to be off twenty miles, give or take. Navigation must be done consistently and accurately. Of course, with the new GPS systems all of the trauma and trial and error can be avoided nowadays. Still…best to know your navigation. Instruments break, fall overboard, go haywire, and sometimes just die.

Unlike Takaroa, the entry to Rangiroa presented no problems, so we anchored up and began our explorations. Rangiroa was so big that we could not see the other side—about seventeen miles across. The side we were on was populated by two small settlements and a resort. We anchored by the resort and enjoyed their bar facilities (they had ice!). Leslie and I, rather piqued by the constant harassment of sharks, did not dive in Rangiroa, but Tom and Larry did. They discovered later that night, while looking through a book, that Rangiroa is the place where major shark research is done, and that the small islet around which they'd been diving is the feeding grounds for hammerheads, tiger sharks, etc. They did not go diving there again either.

We bade farewell to the Tuomotos and headed off for Tahiti and the Society Islands, our last stop in Polynesia, on May 14th. We'd been going to leave the day before with the *Shannon Marie* but the wind had been a strong southeasterly and we'd learned to wait—we were learning finally. The *Shannon Marie* left 24 hours before us, pounded it out and beat us by only three hours to Tahiti.

THE SOCIETIES

FROM THE LOG of the *Cabaret*:

May 14, 1981
 Beautiful morning. Wind out of the S.E. 5 to 10 knots. All systems go. The current in Avatoru Pass is flooding but we should be able to handle it. The sky looks real good in the direction the wind is coming from, so hopefully this will be a good trip.

May 15, 1981
 Good sail last night. A little slow at times but we kept moving. A few minor squalls.
 Overcast today and blowing like a bugger. With double-reefed main and jib running 7.5 to 9 knots. Great sailing but the sea is really picking up. No MP.

May 15, 1981
 Anchored in Papeete at 3:00 A.M. Came in on the range lights. Easy trip in despite reefs and you name it. That part was spooky. Incredible wind all during the night. Seas let up but that might be due to being in the lee of Tahiti.
 Wow! Tahiti! It is neat to be here!!!

125

We spent a week in Papeete doing the sights and shopping. Our few clothes, constantly exposed to sun, heat, and salt, were in sad shape. And ah! To have clean, machine-washed towels and bed linen was sheer joy. We went wild over the abundance of fresh produce and ate like kings for a week. It was as cheap to eat out as it was to cook aboard (well, almost) so we did plenty of eating out and very much enjoyed ourselves.

Our friends rented a car, and we accompanied them one day on a tour of Tahiti, stopping at all the sight seeing places and enjoying their company. They were preparing to leave the *Shannon Marie* to return to Phoenix, and we knew we'd miss their friendship and Larry's great sense of humor.

We bought a huge chunk of beautiful beef at the Sunday market and canned it, as the canned meat we'd suffered through in the Marquesas and Tuomotos had been insufferable. Remember the good old corned beef your Grandma used to make? The canned corn beef available there bears absolutely no resemblance. The cans we got held a substance that was a cross between stringy strands of meat liberally mixed with great globules of a white mucilage-looking stuff and a gelatinous mass that instantly made one's eyes cross and nose pucker. Once we bought a canned ham at great expense that was so bad we ate only half a piece and then threw the rest overboard. I debated on donating it to a needy, vagabond French couple and their two scrawny children, but I honestly felt they'd have thought it was an insult. We caught only one fish between Acapulco and Tahiti, and that had been off Takaroa. We had been hesitant to spear fish since fish poisoning is not unheard of. Only locals were supposedly able to tell the difference between a poisonous and nonpoisonous fish, but I wondered because after all there were no newspapers available to announce natives' deaths and what they died from. We learned that spear fishing was not a wise idea, however, since one day an area could be okay, and the next it could be poisonous. Fish on one side of a lagoon pass could be fine, while the same species on the other side of the pass could be deadly. (This strongly reminded me of the mysterious red tide in Canada that always appears at the start of the boating season...perhaps it is just a way to conserve what is there.) But I wasn't about to challenge local lore. So when we got that gorgeous chunk of beef in Tahiti, I carefully canned it in ½ pint jars with the idea that we'd ration it carefully and make it to Hawaii with plenty to spare. Once we left Tahiti, however, we found the availability of beef was limited, so we broke into our stores earlier than planned.

We made the final decision in Tahiti to begin our homeward bound route. After our meeting with the Olsons in Tahuata, we toyed off and on (more off than on for Tom) with the idea of going to the Cook Islands and then Samoa, but for various reasons in Tahiti we cemented plans to return…we still didn't know where exactly we were returning to, but we at least had made the first big decision and knew we'd have time enroute to decide on the finer points. We loaded up Larry and Leslie's personal belongings from the *Shannon Marie* that they'd been unable to get in with their sixteen pieces of luggage. At least 100 books, blankets, pillows, freeze dried food, diving equipment, and art supplies were among their "donations." We relished all of it, particularly the books. We had started off with a great library but found at book swaps with other boaters that we were about the only people reading a steady diet of classics. Our choices for exchange were often romances, mysteries, or westerns. We always came out on the losing end of the deal in any book exchange.

From Tahiti we ventured the twelve miles to Moorea and anchored in incredibly clear and shallow water in Kia Ora. On our entrance we'd first anchored *Cabaret* in deeper water and then gone in the area by skiff. We decided to take *Cabaret* in then—slowly and carefully. Tom stood at the bow and gave signals to avoid coral heads. I steered with a pounding heart. When we anchored we decided that if there was enough room between the keel and the sandy bottom to swim through then we'd stay. There was a good two foot clearance! My only fear were the "pigfish" creatures that hung around our boat. They looked just like little pigs and looked poisonous.

We went to church on Moorea and had quite an experience. Knowing that we had a big crossing coming up, I got the religious call again (gosh I hate people like myself!) so one Sunday we rowed ashore to a little church whose denomination we didn't know. We entered and were seated but then were immediately asked to sit up in front by the altar—sort of like on display. Tom began to act desperate and kept whispering for us to get out of there.

"Shh. Just act like you know what you're doing," I counseled.

"Come on, Becky. We can slip right out that door. They'll never see us again."

"Be quiet and sit still. Act like you're praying and enjoying yourself," I rejoined.

The service ensued and we were the objects of attention. Neither of us knew a word of what was being spoken, so I sat there and tried to think holy thoughts, hoping the minister was not putting us on display as infidels. The service dragged on. Periodically everybody in the congregation in unison flicked their eyes in our direction and looked us over—I knew then they were talking about us. I tried to look interested—and holy. After the service we were made to stand by the preacher (escorted there by a member of the congregation) and everybody shook hands with us. Some were curious; some seemed hostile. The last two people to leave spoke French and English and explained that we were the first foreign visitors they'd ever had in their church. They asked us to send them hymnals when we returned home so they could have more songs to sing. We sent them later with another boater.

A few days later we moved to Oponu Bay on Moorea and anchored Canadian style to shore. We stayed a few days, swimming and walking and then left for Raiatea, an overnight run. We had a good southeast wind and eventually had to take the genoa down and put the jib up so we could slow down a bit and have a daylight arrival. As it turned out we had to heave to for a few hours anyway. We entered the lagoon in the morning, and for the first time since Alaska actually found a protected little anchorage behind a motu all to ourselves. We tied stern to shore and spent several days lolling and playing on the island.

We stopped at the main island of Raiatea and anchored in the new marina being built. We went shopping and walking about, stopping for meals in interesting looking places. We finally decided to circumnavigate the adjoining island of Tahaa, inside the reef, and then go on to Bora Bora, our last stop in Polynesia. The anchorages in Tahaa, however, proved to be very deep, and our experiences there were nothing short of disappointing. From the Log of the *Cabaret:*

June 3, 1981

Never will I quite believe the events of today! What a nasty day—It would have been worse to be at sea, but that's the only place (I think).

Anyway, it was windier than all get out in our inlet. It was howling and whipping us around. We decided to pull anchor at 8:00 A.M. but could not get it up—we suspected it might be wrapped around coral heads, but thought too that maybe the wind was causing problems.

About 11:00 we tried again. No luck. Tom had to put his tanks on and go down. The anchor was incredibly wrapped up. We got it up and took off in search of a protected bay. Each bay we came to, however, was like a wind funnel! And deep!!

Once we anchored along the passageway but I didn't like it so we moved on. Once we found this little bay and anchored there only to discover two coral heads about 15 feet from us. Finally we decided to go back to Raiatea.

The wind was blowing so hard by this time we could hardly make headway. Finally we realized we could not make Raiatea by dark, so then the race was on to find an anchorage. We at last found a spot where we are quite protected. We are tied stern to shore—bow anchor is in about 60 feet. We'll just stay put till the weather breaks. Tahaa is hardly our favorite spot.

We were stormed in for four days but were so well protected that we had to look through binoculars to check the seas outside the area. We had a good time though, and besides filling our water tanks, showering daily in the deluge, and snorkeling in our protected cove, we explored a bit in the skiff, wrote letters, ate popcorn, and played Scrabble until I felt like screaming...because I always lose...because I am always trying to make the "big" word. Tom comes along with a two letter word that has double word score, triple points, and connects to one of my big words and kills me. No doubt I am a poor loser. It rained and blew heavily the whole time, and we were very glad to be at anchor in a nice spot instead of crashing about at sea. So much for our circumnavigation of Tahaa.

We were finally able to get away and motored in windless conditions to Bora Bora. We anchored at the Bora Bora Yacht Club, of which we became official members, and began our last nine days in Polynesia.

I was very interested in Bora Bora because I had just finished *Hawaii,* by James Michener, and was intrigued with the notion that we'd be taking the very same voyage the ancient Bora Borans had taken when they'd made their trip to Hawaii. Michener had the Bora Borans wanting to stop at Nuku Hiva in the Marquesas, however, which even I felt was rather out of their way, but then I reasoned that maybe they weren't exactly sure where they were going. Anyway, I was thrilled with the idea of making this trek, and subconsciously I figured that if they could do it in a reed boat with few provisions it ought to be a cakewalk for us. I did wonder about their navigating by the north star by using its reflection in a coconut shell filled with water, however, since I'd yet been at sea when it was calm enough to see anything reflected at night in a coconut shell, let alone navigate by it. I told myself it was because the trip was so easy that this could be done. I had my little fantasy dispelled, however, by Louis Valier, a visitor on another boat from Hawaii, who, being an expert navigator and astronomer, informed me that the navigational section of Michener's account of the Bora Borans was fictionalized because the north star was not even there to be used back then.

We rented bicycles in Bora Bora and easily circumnavigated the small island, stopping for lunch and a swim. Tom tried desperately to master a palm tree—something he'd been vainly attempting ever since Mexico—and the pressure was really on him now as soon we'd be out of palm tree territory and back to fir. We'd stop at every tree that looked remotely possible and he'd give it a try. Finally we found one that was not only short, but had a real lean to it. When he got part way up I squatted beneath the tree and took a picture, thus making him look like he was way up there, which of course he was!

We ate ice cream by the quart and drank plenty of beer at the yacht club in an effort to fatten up for the trip (in case it was another bad one and we lost weight). This trying to fatten up was a novel and completely new experience for me, and one I really liked. Our efforts were in vain though, because of our activities I'm sure. We were not boat sitters or loungers, and always within a few days of our arrival in any bay or port had done everything there was to do. A couple of boats had been in Bora Bora three weeks and had not yet ventured into the small town. We had established a daily exercise routine in Mexico and had been pretty faithful in adhering to it (except for the crossings). The routine consisted of a list of calisthenics and several miles of swimming. We did not count walking as part of the exercise program. People were always mortified to see us out on deck doing sit-ups, bends, curl-ups (with the weights from our flopper stoppers) and other things. Many of them thought we were nuts, which of course we somewhat were. I always liked to think that our trying to halfway stay in shape might help save our lives in a moment of desperation. I think it only served to make us an oddity among cruisers, although I did feel better psychologically for at least trying to do something. I often wondered why some boaters had gone to the expense of going so far just to lie around and to read when they could have done so much more reasonably at home.

We finally learned how to shell when a girl at the yacht club mentioned getting out in the morning before the tracks were erased. Mentally I was guffawing my head off over this girl's suggestion that shells left tracks. The next day, Ed Crumbly, off another boat, showed us how to shell...and guess what? You locate a track and swim to the end of it. You plunge you hand into the sand and scoop up a beautiful shell. If you strike out you simply swim to the other end of the track and scoop. In a short time we had a bag full of beautiful marlin spikes to add to our meager collection of cowries.

Although each place we'd gone had had its "characters", Bora Bora seemed to have a few extra. One evening, after spending the afternoon swinging out on the main halyard and diving in, playing the day away like children, we met a very unusual man who had come to Bora Bora from Hawaii on a small powerboat. Needless to say he'd run out of fuel in the trip, had jury rigged a sail, and spent literally days and days wandering about in circles before he found Bora Bora. Not surprisingly his girlfriend jumped ship upon arrival, but he seemed to have no trouble getting others. He sold fish to the yacht club and a few of the local restaurants. He told intriguing stories of water spouts, which introduced a new, potential calamity I'd not thought of before.

Before our departure we went out for a fancy dinner at Bora Bora's resort (sort of a Last Supper). I wore my newly purchased French clothes and one of my newly acquired shell necklaces. We dined sumptuously, knowing this would be the last great meal for a spell, and walked back along the beach to the yacht club. It was a long walk, but it was a perfect South Pacific night and I wanted to hold it for as long as possible. Suddenly I knew what all those WWII veterans had been talking about. The moon was full, the sky clear, a slight breeze, and the island did appear a virtual paradise. It was an exotic night, and I will never forget the moon shining through the palm trees on a radiant white beach. We talked quietly, a torrent of impressions, thoughts and reminiscences of our Polynesian trip coming back. The walk was over too quickly; the specialness gone. Two days later we too were gone. We raised anchor at noon, but unlike the Bora Borans we did not crash out through the reef opening. We raised sail and glided through, altered course, and began another long journey.

HAWAIIAN
INTERLUDE

THE TRIP TO HAWAII was almost totally to windward and was terrible. For most of 21 days we literally crashed our way northward, clawing desperately for all the easting we could get. We were lucky to hold our own. Our original plan had been to land at Hilo on the big island of Hawaii and then to mosey on down the chain of islands, stopping and seeing them all. The prevailing northeast trades and accompanying seas finally beat us down, however, and we simply aimed for Honolulu and gave up on the Hawaiian cruise. We could, in fact, have made it, but by the time we'd beat our way 2,400 miles to the base of the Hawaiin chain, we decided the monstrous beat up the east coast of the island was more than we would want to stand.

Leaving Bora Bora was not easy for me. As I watched the small island gradually diminish I felt a sickening in my stomach. I was not the eager voyager I had been when we left Acapulco. In fact, I got physically sick that first night at sea, sick from the growing sense of doom in my stomach. Fortunately, the first four days out were good days and nights which help immeasurably in our adjustment. The closer we edged to the equator, however, the more squally, windy, and rougher it became. We were no longer on a beam reach, but beating hard with the wind and seas from the northeast. Sometimes

133

Cabaret would fall off a wave so hard that the rigging would shudder, vibrating the whole boat. We dressed a lot warmer than we had in months and held on. We were blessed periodically with beautiful weather, although the wind direction continued to stink, and the further north we got the stronger it got.

From the Log of the *Cabaret*:

June 29, 1981

A nice night ended up in some horrible, horrible squalls from about 5:30 A.M. to noon or better. Hand steering. A million sail changes. H U G E seas. This is disgusting. We can maintain absolutely no easting at all. Losing ground like crazy.

No MP due to clouds. Log shows 95 miles.

4:30 P.M. Heaved to for the night. We are both too tired to go on. We'll get some sleep tonight and tackle it in the A.M. Clearing. Believe we're into the N.E. trades. Oh boy.

June 30, 1981

Very rough and windy night. Heaved to. Got underway at 5:15 A.M. Blowing 30 knots maybe. BIG seas.

Noon MP (very rolly) puts us at 152.20 W and 8.39 N. We're not as far west as we thought—probably thanks to the counter equatorial current.

Hurricane Beatrice is humming up the Mexican coast. Hope it does not head this direction!

Log shows only 45 miles (due to being heaved to).

July 1, 1981

Very windy last night. Went all night on storm sail and reefed main.

Blue skies today but very rough and windy…30+ knots with very lumpy seas that keep drenching us.

Noon MP put us at 10.10 N and 152.52 W. Log shows 95 miles—not bad for not having much canvas up.

Hurricane Beatrice is now at 19N, 116W. Hopefully it will continue on a n.w. route.

We rotated from the berth below to the cockpit, reading almost constantly to try to distract us from the pounding we had to endure, bathing daily still, but forgoing the casino hours for discussion.

A major issue of discussion was our future plan of action. We were debating on wintering in Hawaii and selling the boat, or if not selling it then returning home the next summer. We both dreaded the thought of another passage—especially right after the one we were on, hence our idea of wintering in Hawaii. This seemed a real reasonable idea to us, but just in case the boat sold right off we also tried to decide where we wanted to live when we returned to the mainland. Tom was heavily in favor of the San Juans or Portland. I was in favor of Alaska or Newport. Each place had so many pros and so few cons that it was hard to make a decision. Sometimes to help us feel better I'd say, "Well, Tom, where don't we want to live?" We then knew we only wanted to live in the Northwest, not California, Texas, Florida, Kansas, New York, Nebraska or any of the other states. So we weren't as undecided as we thought we were. Tom knew his goal upon returning was to go into business for himself, something he'd been dreaming about since we'd first gone to Alaska. He wanted his own boat shop. He spent hours at night on watch making lists of tools and needs, designing his shop, and setting up his business. I had no such driving goal. Maybe I would return to teaching, I mused, a job I simultaneously loved and hated. I had written the school where I'd last taught four years previous when we left Bora Bora asking if a job might be available. It was a chance in a million, I knew, of course, but as I told Tom, we might as well get at least one iron in the fire. We had all of $600 left to our name. I had told them in the letter that we were on our way home, and I'd appreciate being considered for any job that might become available. I told them they could write to me in care of the Hawaii Yacht Club as we'd be in Hawaii in July. Tom simply told me I was nuts.

And so passed our days bouncing northward, wondering how in the hell the Bora Borans could ever have navigated by using a star's reflection in a coconut gourd. Our nights were spent huddled beneath the dodger reading and, I'm ashamed to say, sleeping. I slept through a good portion of my watches on that passage and I don't know why. I was terrified of running into ships, but I guess I was more tired than scared. I knew the area was not in the big shipping lanes, and I knew there were no atolls lurking in the dark, and so when Tom would wake me for watch I simply stumbled from one prone position to another most nights. Nights I did not sleep or read, my thoughts would drift homeward, or back to Alaska. It's not hard to daydream about a dream, and our two year adventure in Alaska had seemed like the greatest dream-come-true I'd ever had. Since I was a child, and for no reason I know of, Alaska was like a steady rhythm in my fantasies. So my days and nights filled with these still cherished dreams, I felt stronger than ever the pull to return. Perhaps it had been the zenith of our travels.

The days crept by along with the miles. At times we gritted our teeth at the terrific beating of wind and sea. Our only mishaps were when BIG JOHN, our wind vane, broke midway, when a snap shackle gave way in a squall, and when Tom developed an infected arm from a bug bite. We remedied the BIG JOHN loss by turning the steering over to Tilly. Neither of us felt the small contraption could handle it since BIG JOHN had broken due to so much torque from the heavy seas, but she certainly did. The snap shackle was replaced with a spare, but Tom's arm scared us both. We were about seven days out of Bora Bora when the swelling and feverishness in it became very noticeable. We tried cold packs and aspirin for a day or two but it continued to get worse. Finally I broke out our Mexican antibiotics and started Tom on them. I had no idea how often he needed to take them, so I gave him four pills a day for six days. Unbeknownst to him I read up in our First Aid Afloat and knew that some people go into shock with antibiotics. I was scared to death that this might happen to Tom and didn't know what I'd do if it did happen as we had no adrenalin medication to administer. I watched him carefully and surreptitiously for an hour after he took the first pill and was greatly relieved when he showed no signs of a reaction. I knew that six days was probably not long enough to be on the medicine, but there was nothing I could do about it. I figured it would take at least two days for the arm to get bad again after the pills were all taken if it was going to get worse, and then within two more days I was sure I could raise help in Hawaii somehow. I figured we were safe. The medicine seemed to work—the arm improved. He lived.

From the Log of the *Cabaret*:

July 6, 1981

Windier than a bugger last night! We finally had to take the jib down and put up storm sail and double reefed main. Still hit 9 knots on the gusts. Wind was pretty strong this A.M. but has practically died on us. We are now motoring.

Noon MP puts us at 156.37W and 19.26 N. This agrees almost exactly with Tom's DR and visual fix on Hawaii.

Yes! We are in sight of land. Saw lights last night and the island became visible at dawn. Sure makes me feel good about my navigation!

Log shows 110 miles run, but noon to noon makes 138. Should be in Honolulu tomorrow night! Fortunately we have lots of fuel left so that should be no problem.

Our last night at sea was a memorable one no doubt. We motored until 6:00 P.M. then began sailing. We were out of the lee of Hawaii and entering the funnel of Alenuihaha Channel. There is nothing very "ha ha" about it. The wind howled as we violently rocked beam to 10 to 12 foot seas all night. With only a double reefed main we rolled hideously, running water into the low side of the cockpit. Neither of us could sleep when off watch, so we huddled all night in the cockpit, bracing our legs on the lower seat and hoping the misery would soon end. Below decks was total chaos. Books that had comfortably and snugly beat and bounced their way across thousands of miles of sea were thrown out of their racks and were strewn everywhere. The silverware drawer emptied itself with a hideous clatter because it was not completely shut, and in general the night was a last minute vicious reminder of what I hated about passages.

We made landfall at 7:30 the following evening, immediately espied Ron and Nancy on *Columbine*, a boat we'd met in our travels in Canada and later San Diego, and felt right at home on good old terra firma.

We both called home that night, collect of course, and talked to our parents for the first time in ages. My mother was happy to hear from us and anxious to know our plans. So were we.

The next day we moved to the Hawaii Yacht Club and called immigration. They were indignant that we'd not called immediately upon our arrival and viewed us quite suspiciously. They came to our boat; one took Tom off for paperwork, and the other stayed aboard with me. I watched him as he nosed about peering into the most peculiar places. He asked few questions and finally I told him that if he'd tell me exactly what he was looking for then maybe I could help him find it. He merely answered, "Let's just say you've been to some places we view as having a great deal of suspicious drug activity."

"Mexico and Polynesia, you mean?"

"Ah, yes, one might say Mexico and Tahiti."

"Oh," I meekly answered.

Suddenly, as I watched him tasting dust that had embarrassingly gathered under the mattress, my eyes bugged out as I realized he was straddling our "emergency" bucket. This was a bucket of emergency supplies we always kept ready in case we had to abandon the boat for our skiff (heaven forbid). It contained sunglasses, suntan oil, a spare harmonica, fishing tackle, bandaids, knives, flare gun, and... our Mexican antibiotics for which we had no prescription since you can purchase anything over the counter in Mexico. I didn't know whether to be quiet and hope he didn't open it, or whether to say, "Oh, here, is this what you want? You can have them now—we're safe." I was paralyzed with indecision and simply stared in fear as he continued to poke and sniff around, always straddling the bucket or touching it with his leg.

We were admonished, but admitted back into the United States after we promised we had not dumped any garbage upon our arrival or left the boat. I didn't think our using the phone that was ten feet away really counted like having gone in for dinner would have.

Our first stop in Honolulu was McDonald's, where we relished our quarterpounders with cheese, fries and strawberry milkshakes like it was a glutinous orgy. Our next stop was at a boat broker's office where we listed the boat and hoped for an immediate sale. As I eyed all the boats for sale on his wall, however, I realized that we weren't the only ones who got to Hawaii with that thought in mind.

We spent our first week trying to get the salt spray off the boat, sprucing up the bright work, and trying to get things shipshape again. We enjoyed ourselves at the yacht club too and were treated great by the people there. The Trans Pac came in while we were there which added to the excitement and bustle of the whole waterfront area. We met with former Mexico boaters, had dinner with Louis Valieur whom we'd met in Bora Bora, and met Jack and Dorothy Hoyle from San Diego, who treated us to breakfast. Jack had a boat in San Diego and was very interested in our boat. We spent some time with Ron and Nancy on *Columbine* and we made new friends with Siggy and Maria Kemmler on *Tanager*, hailing from British Columbia. We really enjoyed their friendship and saw a lot of them before we left Hawaii.

Yes. We left Hawaii. It was soon all too apparent that the market there was flooded with boats. And once Tom was back in the northern hemisphere he was too fired up to get started in his own business and didn't want to "fritter away" a year in Hawaii odd jobbing it on boats. We still didn't know where we were going for sure. We knew where we weren't going (Texas, Florida, New York, etc.) but we had not yet made up our minds about the Northwest. I got a letter from the school I'd written to saying there were no jobs available but if something came along they'd keep me in mind. Well, it had been worth a try. A long shot.

We left Honolulu after two weeks of fixing up the boat, playing tourist, and eating out three times a day, and headed for Pokai Bay after one night at the incredibly noisy Keehi Lagoon. If I'd had any inclination to live aboard in Hawaii, the experience of listening to jets and military bombers all day and night did it in for me.

We spent a day at Pokai Bay with Siggy and Maria and their son Robert and then left for Hanalei Bay on Kauai, the home of Puff the Magic Dragon and the usual jumping off point for boats heading back to the mainland. Siggy and Maria headed on to another port and circumnavigated Kauai. We saw them again though when they showed up in Hanalei and took us touring in their rented car.

Hanalei Bay was filled with returning Trans Pac boats and a few small (by comparison) cruisers like ourselves. We stayed for a week, diving in what felt like cold water (compared to what we'd gotten used to) and hiking and hitching around. Hanging like a cloud over our visit, however, was the impending trip. Naturally I insisted we go to church again the Sunday before we left. We reprovisioned and topped off our water the day before our scheduled departure. I sent a brief note back to the school telling them I was on my way home, and just in the remote event something became available I gave them my mom's phone number.

We left July 28th, and once outside the protection of the bay the wind caught us abeam and *Cabaret* literally leaped forward, almost seeming to sense that this would be her last passage, her last endurance test with us. We were going home.

WELCOME HOME, CABARET

CABARET HEADED NORTH with a determination I had never felt in the boat before. Despite my being sick again the first night out, all was going well. Four days out of Hawaii, however, we saw the ominous signs of an impending super storm forming to the west. We altered course to the east to try and avoid it as much as possible, and our tactic worked. That night we were treated to the most spectacular lightning display I've ever seen. Continuous flashes ran the length of the horizon to the south and west of us. It was an unparalleled light show, and I was glad I was not in the middle of it.

We had several consistent 125 mile days under jib alone. The barometer was sky high, yet we were experiencing very windy conditions. On August 6th we had a ship alter course and hunt us down in the dark and driving rain. Suddenly, light as bright as day enveloped us when the ship turned its spotlight on us. Like a fool I turned our radio to channel 6 instead of 16, so we were not able to talk with them. We stood in the cockpit in the glaring light, howling wind, driving rain and lumpy seas and waved. After a few minutes the light was extinguished and Tom was able to make out the outline of gun turrets on the bow of the ship.

I think they just wanted to see what a couple of fools looked like, but Tom was worried they were Russians and might use us for target practice.

By August 11th we were slowing and motoring more due to the Pacific High. We had sporadic wind for several days—never anything heavy or squally—weather suited for our genoa and full main. We spent a week becalmed or making only ten miles a day. There was no question that of all the passages we'd made, this trip home was the easiest. This last passage seemed a real luxury also what with the abundance of tuna that we caught and ate like epicureans. The northern latitudes definitely offered the best fishing. We escaped the gales that were forming in the higher latitudes and slept through the calms. I had always wondered how on earth a person could just shut down out in the middle of the ocean and go to bed and just drift all night long. It was easy. We turned on our anchor light and hoped that we'd be visible to ships and went to sleep. I was amazed at myself, for in the past I just could not conceive of ever being able to just drift silently in the middle of thousands of miles of ocean. I thought of it sort of like drifting in space. I think it may be sort of like that. Out of boredom Tom slipped the aquadory off the foredeck, put the 4 horse Johnson on and towed *Cabaret* until he ran out of gas.

While the weather was the most storm free we'd ever had, it was also about the coldest we'd known in ages. We weren't even two days out of Hawaii when Tom announced he was going to put on his long underwear.

"Tom, you've got to wait until we at least get to 35N! You'll be dead by 40N if you put them on now!"

"It's freezing out here, Becky. I'll be alright. I'll wear two pair at 40N."

"What two pair, Tom? Remember in your ecstasy to leave Alaska how you flung almost all your long underwear overboard when we crossed Dixon Entrance? I told you that you'd be sorry!"

Silence. Two days later we were both wearing long underwear. Tom donned his gray woolies and I dug out my cotton pair. With sweat pants, a wool hat, and my sweater and float coat on I managed to survive. Needless to say the bathing hour slipped by each day unheeded. Finally I agreed to heat water in kettles and take a warm bath only. When I slipped out of my costume, however, I was appalled to see a molting body. "There goes my South Pacific tan!"

I cried. Tom too was "molting", and we wondered if we'd have any tan left at all when we got home.

Tom still suckered me one day, however, when we were becalmed. He nonchalantly stripped down, dived overboard, and began soaping up.

"Isn't that water cold, Tom?"

"No! It feels great! You ought to try it!"

"Thanks, but I'll stick to warm baths!"

"No, really, Becky. It feels good. You'll like it. You'll feel a lot better."

I eyed him suspiciously and watched as he soaped again and dove over the side.

"You comin' in, or are you getting old?"

"No...I don't...oh well. Yeah. I'll do it. Are you *sure* it's warm?" I shivered just looking at the water. I waited for him to climb out, rinse off with warm water and dry off. We never both went in at the same time lest for some reason the boat took off.

"Okay! Here I go!" One last pause. "Are you *sure* it's not cold, Tom?"

"Go ahead! It feels good!"

Reluctantly I stood on the rail and looked at the flat, calm water. Well, it stood to reason the water must be warm or there wouldn't be albacore in it, right? Here goes nothing!

I leaped. I remember my blood racing backwards and my heart stopping as my breath escaped, leaving me gasping and swinging paralyzed arms trying to regain the quickly drifting boat. I latched on to the steering vane rudder with numb hands and jerkily pulled myself up. No voice yet.

"It's amazing how fast the boat is drifting, isn't it?" Tom laughingly asked.

"You! You said it was warm!" Now it was all coming back to me. I had forgotten somehow that this was the weird-o who jumped overboard all throughout our travels in Alaska and Canada. He was still laughing.

"Fooled you!"

I washed since I was totally numb by then and no longer in pain, climbed out, and half-heartedly had to admit I did feel refreshed.

We used fresh water more freely than ever before because it was not really potable. We had topped off our tank in Hanalei and apparently had done it when the well was too low or something, for two days out of Hanalei I noticed the water tasted more hideous than anything I'd ever drunk. In addition it was thick with floating particles. We were able to use it for cooking, washing, and rinsing our mouths after brushing, but to drink it was almost impossible. Fortunately, we had a huge supply of juices and we also had a five gallon jerry jug of water that we always carried for emergency purposes. We ended up with about one thermos of water left by landfall.

I canned tuna until I finally ran out of jars. Upon our return I was giving my canned tuna away by the dozen until I opened a jar one day to make some sandwiches. It was pure gold compared to store bought; I immediately regretted my former generosity.

Like our previous passages we spent time almost everyday trying to decide where we were going to settle down. We both agreed that if we did choose Alaska, we did not want to live aboard again, so we early on knew our landfall would be Oregon. Tom was still sold on either Portland or Puget Sound as a future home. I was still for Newport, Wrangell, or Puget Sound, in that order. We went back to the pros and cons and finally eliminated Wrangell and Alaska because of the distance from our families. Our travels had given us an appreciation for familial ties that I'd never before felt. I kept my faith in Newport, but agreed I could probably live pretty happily just about anywhere.

This trip I spent my time on watch being alert, for we saw ships almost daily. We learned that if I called the ships we got a really nice response from the radioman. When Tom called, a gruff voice would only give monosyllabic answers. I'd call and try to sound like a dingbat cheesecake (not a stretch for me—the ding bat part, I mean) and I seemed to get a lot more discussion going. The ships affirmed our fixes, gave us weather reports, and frequently seemed curious about what I was doing out there in the middle of nowhere. One officer called us back and when he found out we had no radio other than VHF, he asked us if we wanted him to call someone on the mainland and let them know our location and E.T.A. I gave him my mother's phone number. Five minutes later he called back to tell us he'd reached her and she was so happy to hear that we were okay. Later I was glad we'd chosen my mother to be contacted as I learned that that very day she had been told my step-father had terminal cancer...and the previous day she had buried her sister, my Aunt Joe. She had needed some good news.

We had been in Tahiti when I first received word that my aunt was dying, and I began to spend a great deal of time thinking about her, dying at 49, alone, and with so much unspoken sorrow and disappointment with her life's lot. I seemed to have most memories of my Aunt Joe when we were younger and I would visit her for a few weeks every summer. Summers seemed so much longer and hotter in those days! She and I would go to a deliciously cold, air-conditioned restaurant for lunch and eat all we could for 99 cents. I always got carried away eating beets! But it was perfect to go there with her in her old jalopy and sit together in the cold, dark environs filling ourselves with endless selections of food.

She introduced me to the worlds of science fiction, perfect spaghetti sauce, and the most wonderful salmon loaf. Her brick and board bookcase was loaded with great sci-fi, and long before I was even in junior high I was well read in Ray Bradbury and Isaac Asimov. We both loved creepy movies and spooky things and would go to the drive-in movies to watch horror flicks.

My aunt was always wonderfully slender. Her beautifully freckled face had a Huckleberry Finn charm, and her humor was warm. She would sit at the piano and her long fingers instinctively found the right chords and keys. Her piano playing was spontaneous. Mine was always so studied and rote. We'd always gather around and sing out songs like "It Had to Be You," "Birth of the Blues, and "You Made Me Love You." Such were my thoughts on my long trek across the Pacific Ocean to where my aunt lay dieing. And I found myself alone at night, murmuring aloud under the brilliant Pacific stars, murmuring and muttering to myself in protestation, "Joe, Joe, the world goes on, you know." Every night I cried.

Other contacts we had at sea were with the *Ondine* and *Columbine*, and the *Billy Marie II*. The *Ondine* heard us calling the Astoria marine operator. We were still over 500 miles away from Astoria but were picking up radio skips. It was music to our ears. Naturally our VHF could not reach Astoria, but it did reach the *Ondine* on a skip of over one hundred miles. They told us they'd heard *Cabaret* called on the radio literally all day the day before. The *Ondine* disagreed with my position and maintained we were much further north and west. I knew I was correct, however, as after three passages and the Tuomotos I had great confidence in my navigational ability. They insisted they were correct. When we lost radio contact with them I knew we'd both been correct as we'd simply had a skip again.

Columbine motored past us on one of our becalmed days, and I have to admit I was envious that we didn't have a bigger fuel supply. We chatted with them and watched them slowly disappear into the fog. I found it interesting that our paths crossed out in the middle of nowhere.

The *Billy Marie II* hailed us one morning on the radio, for he saw our sails in the distance. I talked with the skipper for some time, mentioning that we had to reserve our last four inches of fuel to get in over the bar and into Astoria in case there was no wind. I could not believe my ears when he offered to drop us five gallons of diesel. I gladly took him up on his offer, and soon we saw two tuna boats steaming towards us. The *Billy Marie* pulled in front of our slowly sailing craft and dropped a five gallon jug attached to a bright buoy off his stern. We retrieved the fuel and knew it was one lucky day.

We were also able to finally reach the marine operator that day, and I called my mom. She was glad to know we were almost home and promised to call Tom's parents and let them know of our arrival. "Oh, by the way," she added, the secretary from Taft High School called and said there was a last minute opening in English. If you're interested you're supposed to call as soon as possible."

Was this really happening? My one iron in the fire would bear heat? We were headed towards Astoria and then Portland—should we head to Newport instead? A million questions suddenly arose.

"Should I go for it, Tom?"

"I don't know, Becky. Do what you want. What do you think?"

"I don't know, Tom. What if I get the job? How will you feel about living in Newport?"

"I don't know, Becky. I honestly don't know," he answered somewhat reluctantly.

Tom was not jubilant over this news, but I figured I might as well try for the job. I could always turn it down if I needed to. We had only $600 to our name, and how could I refuse the possibility of a year's worth of paychecks? It would get us on our feet again if nothing else.

I located the marine operator and put a call through to Bobbi Schiemann, my long time friend and the school secretary. "Get here as soon as you can, Becky," was all she could say.

As if this was not good enough as it was, the wind continued to increase in strength, and by that night we were flying under jib alone averaging seven knots.

Our landfall was as dramatic as one could expect. Our last day at sea found us in heavy overcast. We could see no land as we approached the coast. A fishing vessel gave us our location as 20 miles west of Cape Disappointment. Tom, using RDF exclusively, had us as precisely located as he could. A short time later we picked up the diaphone in medium fog and headed in. All morning I had been monitoring the VHF, and I was horrified to hear the Coast Guard locating the remains of several drowned fishermen. The conditions of the bar were deadly, yet where we were seemed so calm. Suddenly the Coast Guard announced on Channel 16 that the bar would be closed to traffic until further notice.

"Bullshit!" I exploded. "After what I've been through nobody is making me spend another night out here!"

"Becky, we can't go in if it's closed."

"Of course we can. What can they do to us? Arrest us? Well, they can come and arrest me gladly!" I was really getting excited. "Tom, I'm not spending another night out here. This is ridiculous. We have crossed 7,000 miles of ocean just to get back home! Now! I'm going in!!"

Tom agreed, and so we continued on our route. As we motored in calm seas I wondered how on earth they could close the bar when there were so many small boats beginning to appear. I knew that people would die of hypothermia if forced to stay out all night in small open craft, so I felt assured they'd open the bar again.

About a mile later the south jetty became visible, and we cheered and began singing away as we watched the outline of land appear in the foggy distance. Happily the Coast Guard reopened the bar as we approached it. It was as calm as I'd ever seen it. We proceeded along the interminable string of buoys that leads to Astoria, suddenly feeling so much older and wiser. I could not help but think about our first forays out of that monstrous man-eating bar, and I thought of the years and experiences we'd had since then. I felt like a returning veteran. It was then that I realized we had not really been sailors when we left on our trip. We had been people who sailed, yes, but we had not been true sailors a year ago. We were coming home sailors, however. We had had our butts kicked around the Pacific Ocean, but we came home on our own boat—not a 747. The trip home seemed easy, but perhaps that was because we had learned to anticipate bad weather thereby avoiding the worst storms, and determine what was appropriate sail to carry before it was too late. I trusted my navigational abilities completely. Had I not predicated Nuku Hiva? The Big Island? Cape Disappointment? We were confident. We had become passage makers.

We docked in Astoria August 23, 1981, at 5:45 P.M., one year to the day and almost minute that we'd left from Newport headed south. We could not have planned it more exactly if we'd tried.

The next day we refilled the *Billy Marie II's* jug of diesel and returned it. We thanked them profusely, for we knew our landfall in calm winds and seas was made so much more possible with their help. We headed *Cabaret* up river and made that pastoral trip jubilantly. Enroute our radio came alive with a call for us from Sauvies Island, where Tom's parents had been patiently awaiting our arrival. That night, unable to make Sauvies Island by dark, we stopped in Rainier. In the growing dark we saw two familiar faces as Tom's parents greeted us. We spent most of the night talking with them. In the morning, surprised to see a huge tug tied in front of us (since we'd not heard a sound nor felt a move) we slipped away and soon were heading up Multnomah Channel to our Sauvies Island Moorage. One last bend and it finally came into view. As we approached we could see a huge sign, "Welcome Home, *Cabaret.*" I could not help but remember lines from a Robert Louis Stevenson poem, "Home is the sailor, home from the sea." Yes, indeed. Welcome home, *Cabaret.*